"Remember those favorite teachers who guided, encouraged, pushed and nurtured you to succeed? Now they've written a book to equip and empower you to STEAM-powered success. Read it. Heed it. It could change your life!"
— John R. Hall, PE, F.NSPE, Past-President of the Florida Engineering Society, Framer of Florida's STEM Strategic Plan and President of Ludovici & Orange Consulting Engineers

"This is a guide for our girls to succeed on every level: personally, socially, educationally, professionally and even romantically. The authors detail a system of problem solving that works. I wish I had read this back in the day. Now, I'll make sure that all of the young ladies in my life get a copy. Thanks, Lizzy and Nola!"
— Susan M. Klock, Attorney, mother and grandmother

"This book is timely, long overdue, and reaches the hearts and minds of our future female leaders. The advice and tools are both informative and empowering to young women and will aid them in their career growth."
— M. Lewis Temares, PhD, Dean Emeritus, College of Engineering, University of Miami, IEEE Life Senior Member, and IT and Leadership Consultant, Lew and Lou Consulting LLC

"A great resource to encourage, equip and empower young girls interested in STEAM education and careers. It is full of real-world stories and practical advice from women who have been there. Highly recommended."
— Greg Munson, Founder and President, BattleBots

"Nola and Lizzy have found a way to integrate effective tools for a successful journey through the difficult teen years and beyond. Even girls who are not interested in STEAM careers can benefit from the tech savvy advice in these pages."
— Fon Davis, Founder of Fonco Studios, worked on over 40 feature films, Robogames and Battlebots judge

STEAM POWERED GIRLS

POWER YOUR
DREAMS

POWER YOUR
FUTURE!

STEAM POWERED GIRLS

ELIZABETH DE ZULUETA AND NOLA GARCIA DE QUEVEDO

Power Your Dreams Publishing

STEAM Powered Girls

Published by Power Your Dreams Publishing
Learn more at www.steampoweredgirlsbooks.com

ISBN (paperback): 978-1-7361268-0-6
ISBN (ebook): 978-1-7361268-1-3

Edited by Jessica Vineyard, Red Letter Editing, www.redletterediting.com
Book design by Christy Collins, Constellation Book Services

Printed in the United States of America

DEDICATION

For my best friend and the love of my life, my husband,
William "Billy" Garcia de Quevedo. —Nola

For my mom, Monica De Zulueta, for teaching me to
always strive for my dreams. —Lizzy

And for all of the STEAM-powered girls who read this book.

Contents

ACKNOWLEDGMENTS

I, Nola, would like to thank my best friend and husband, William "Billy" Garcia de Quevedo, for loving me and supporting all of my ideas, dreams, and crazy projects, ever since I fell in love with him when I was sixteen years old. Thank you, Billy, for so many wonderful, adventurous years.

I, Lizzy, would like to thank all of the women who have inspired me along the way and who keep inspiring me every day. A very special thanks goes to my mom, Monica De Zulueta, who taught me that anything is possible as long as you have good time management, and to always choose the hard thing, since that is what teaches us the most about what we are capable of. You are the most brilliant, hardworking, determined, and caring woman I know. Thank you for supporting me in all that I do.

This book is the culmination of four years of work. Many women willingly and courageously donated their time, personal stories, and resources for the book. The questions they were willing to answer in order to give girls the tools to get through challenging times in their lives were personal and not necessarily easy. We thank and commend each and every one of these women for their candor and willingness to show how to deal with challenges that face girls of today and tomorrow, regardless of social circumstances. (You can read about these incredible and inspiring women in appendix A, "Meet Our STEAM-Powered Women.")

We would like to thank the team who guided us through the process of planning, developing, and organizing the content for this book along all of its various stages, and getting it to print. Publishing consultant and book coach Martha Bullen has been a strong force in keeping us aligned with our goals, and referred us to the professional and kind women who filled roles we didn't even know we needed. Developmental and copy editor Jessica Vineyard was exceptionally patient with us, and kindly led us down the path we wanted to go but couldn't always see clearly. Book designer Christy Collins translated our ideas for cover design and put the book into professional and proper order. Our entire publishing team ended up being all women.

Some people say that it is difficult for women to work together, but this book is a testament to the opposite. With their help, we were able to produce a final product that represents all that we want to pass along to the young women who will someday be our local, national, and world leaders. We know that they are unique, each with their own gifts and talents, and filled with potential to be and do whatever they can imagine.

Although this book is dedicated to empowering young women, it is by no means intended to diminish the importance of men. We want to acknowledge the men we have worked with in engineering and robotics, who always treated us as equals and shared their knowledge, ideas, and full support for the projects we undertook, separately and together. The balance of male-female teamwork in STEAM, and in every other endeavor, is a rich and positive thing.

We would like to specifically thank the owners of BattleBots, Trey Roski and Greg Munson, for all they have done to empower female robot builders, and for inspiring so many girls to choose careers in engineering and robotics. Tony Norman and Bob Mimlitch, the founders of VEX Robotics, have positively impacted girls through robotics around the world, from kindergarten through university, by creating opportunities for them to create and compete using their imaginations and intelligence. Trey and Greg, Tony and Bob, thank you for the impact you have made, independently and through your collaborations.

We also thank the many engineering societies across the country who have made a great effort in getting more girls excited about STEAM careers, including the Society of Women Engineers (SWE) and Girl Scouts of America, who have stepped up their game in positively influencing girls in choosing careers that previously had been male dominated.

We would like to acknowledge and thank the many women and girls who have inspired and influenced us. Our sisters, mothers, aunts, cousins, friends, mentors, and teammates have shown us how to maneuver in this world and express ourselves as STEAM-powered women. The multitude of girls and women we have worked with in engineering, robotics, educational programs, and life itself have impacted us in ways that are too numerous to list, but here are a few: the times they refused to give up, the many ways they handled challenging situations, and their willingness to find solutions to practically impossible problems.

And finally, thank you to our readers. Our hope is that you will be positively impacted in such a way that you will live your lives fully, be true to your potential, and be filled with happiness and joy as you make your way as leaders. Thank you.

Preface

Nola's Story

My co-author Lizzy and I both grew up in Miami, but I am a few decades older than she is. Our childhood stories are as different as night and day. I tell you this because a common theme throughout this book, and the responses from all of the women we interviewed, reflect the same message: no matter what happens to us or around us, each of us has the potential, the choice, and the opportunity to be happy and make a great life with the gifts we have inside of us. We are the ones who choose to be great or mediocre; we are the ones who choose to either be a victim of our circumstances or to see our circumstances as opportunities to be the best version of ourselves. We are the ones who can choose to be STEAM-powered girls.

I grew up with seven brothers and sisters from the same parents. Both of my parents were severely alcoholic and abusive. Fortunately, we all had wonderful guardian angels that kept us going—and I really believe in angels.

I went to Catholic schools for twelve years and got a strong, well-rounded, disciplined education. In high school I was voted "Most Likely to Succeed" by my fellow classmates. I look back and wonder what they saw in me that I didn't see at the time, but as I've lived and accomplished the many things I have, I'm so grateful that they did. I am grateful for their belief in me, because remembering that honor bolstered my confidence in my ability to do some extraordinary things.

At the time there weren't a lot of books around that addressed people's potential, and there was not a paradigm that supported the idea that girls could do anything or be anything they dreamed of. Thankfully, I was surrounded by people who believed in me and supported me in pursuing my passions and, occasionally, my crazy ideas that turned into successful projects.

I was at the top of my class; not the valedictorian but up with the smarties. I was offered scholarships to some of the top schools in the country, but life does not always go according to plan, as you either already know or will soon find out. I had fallen deeply in love with an amazing guy, and I chose to get married first and then go to college. I'm still happily married to that amazing guy; we have two awesome sons, a terrific daughter-in-law, and two delightful young granddaughters. They are part of the reason I wanted to write this book.

One year after I graduated, I was diagnosed with severe rheumatoid arthritis (RA). Honestly, I had always thought that RA was an old person's disease, but I was wrong. Now, many years and more than forty surgeries later, I am grateful to be alive and able to do what most people do, with the exceptions of skiing, running, and climbing ladders. I am also now bionic: I have artificial knees, shoulders, hips, and finger joints, and plates in my spine, wrists, and one arm. I am blessed to be surrounded by awesome, interesting, and kind people who are living inspiring lives.

I have also had a couple of strokes. After the second one I decided to go back to college to make sure I was still relatively smart, even though I was almost forty. I got all A's and then decided that instead of finishing college and getting a degree, I would rather use my time volunteering. I started by helping young students make peanut butter and jelly sandwiches for the homeless.

Then our oldest son wanted to join the robotics team at school; it was 1997, and there were few choices for robot teams. I knew very little about robotics and engineering, but I had studied psychology in college and could cook and bake really well, so I thought, I can contribute by making brownies! As it often does, life presented me with a lot of opportunities to raise money for the teams, organize robotics events, and mentor teams with their nontechnical chores. As time went on, just from being around the robots and the kids, and helping out where I was needed, I started learning about robots, their parts and how different things work together. When the opportunity came up to be the head of the first all-female team on the popular television show BattleBots, I jumped at the chance.

Doing that show was the hardest *and* the most fun thing I had ever done. I was working at Florida International University College of Engineering, and my friend Mercy, who was an electrical engineer, agreed to be my partner on Team Fembot, our team on BattleBots. We were the only females in the pits, where the male robot builders were working on their robots between matches. Although the guys were nice and polite, it wasn't until Mercy and I won our first match that they accepted us as equals. When we got back to the pit area after we won our match, the guys stopped working on their robots and gave us a standing ovation. It was truly a powerful moment for us.

Since then, I have produced many local, state, national, and international robotics and STEM events. I and my husband, who is the coolest, kindest, funniest guy I know, have taught at all-girls schools, public schools, private schools, charter schools, and home schools. We have had thousands of students participate in robotics and engineering competitions, STEM projects, and summer camps. Each student has the potential to be one of the many technologically literate leaders needed to find solutions to the many challenges facing us on this planet.

My co-author, Lizzy, was one of the many young women who participated in robotics with us throughout high school. She is a brilliant, kind, multitalented woman who is a joy to work with. She embodies all the qualities of a woman who has integrated the tools of STEAM— science, technology, engineering, the arts, and mathematics—into her life. She has faced challenges in a male-dominated field by learning how to operate as a strong, powerful woman who is able to logically address any challenge that she comes across. She knows how to use STEAM in personal and professional relationships while keeping her integrity intact. When I approached her about co-authoring this book, she was excited to join me. She is a great partner to work with.

I am grateful to the many women who supported the idea to write a book for girls by their willingness to answer intimate questions regarding their formative years and their life experiences. I know that we have put together a book that reminds girls and young women that they are not alone in their experiences, that they are absolutely unique, and that they have everything they need to thrive and succeed in life right inside themselves.

Lizzy's Story

I grew up in Miami, Florida. My parents are both engineers and instilled a love of science into both my brother and me. Ironically, my mom says she never thought I was going to become an engineer because I have such a big personality. She thought I was going to be an actress or a dancer. I do love to dance, and it is still my favorite pastime; however, I have never taken a theater class in my life. My parents love science and engineering so much that whenever they saw a fun project or experiment, they would turn it into a family activity and do the project with my brother and me.

My mom is very hardworking. She has a bachelor's degree, two masters' degrees, and a PhD. She had only her bachelor's degree when she started working, got married, and had two children, and my brother and I were under the age of five when she finished her first master's. Whenever she needed to both study and put us to bed, she would read aloud from her engineering textbooks in the same voice one would use when reading a children's bedtime story. Later, when I asked her how she did it all, she said, "You can read a baby anything if you read it in a nice voice."

My brother and I are only fourteen months apart, which means we are very close and the best of friends, but we were incredibly competitive as little kids. When we got older, my mom would give each of us a textbook, go to a certain page, and ask us to read it to see who could read and understand it faster. The possibility of bragging rights, and being able to show our mom how smart we were, kept us busy while she studied. The reality was that we didn't understand any of it, but it was always fun. It was how my mom showed us that the fun is in the challenge itself and that it doesn't matter if you don't understand it at the end of that day; what matters is trying again the next day. I am happy to say that twenty years later, my brother, who is also an engineer, and I now understand what those books were about.

My mom loved showing us the challenge, the grit, and the thrill of engineering and solving problems. The way she looks at engineering reminds me of a private investigator solving a puzzle. My dad, on the other hand, showed us the wonder of engineering. He is an aeronautical engineer, and whenever an airplane or a helicopter flew by, he would explain to us the history and origin of one part or another, or how the airplane worked and how its wings helped it fly, or how a helicopter's propellers worked to lift it straight up.

Most of my childhood was spent seeing science and engineering all around me and finding out that there was always something fascinating to discover and learn. This is how I was first introduced to building, fabrication, and the creativity and skills engineers must use to build crazy things.

When I was little, my dad's favorite shows were BattleBots and Junkyard Wars. The three of us would sit on the couch, glued to the TV as we watched the BattleBots builders put their robots to the test in the ring, or watched the Junkyard Wars contestants test their creativity when they tried to build a great solution for their given task from just the materials in a junkyard. These shows sparked my obsession with the idea of being able to build anything I could imagine.

I finally got my chance when I entered high school. On the first day of freshman orientation, I wandered into the school's auditorium and saw a bunch of signs for Bots IQ. I immediately called my dad and told him that my school had a BattleBots team and that I had to join. Since the robotics team was so large—it consisted of ninety girls during my time there—they were always looking for parents who were engineers or had machining experience to help as advisors. Since my dad is an engineer and had experience working as a mechanic, he jumped at the chance. I was incredibly excited.

Another great thing that happened when I joined the team was that I met Nola. She and her husband, Bill, owned the machine shop that my school's robotics team worked in. I learned so much during my time working in their shop. I learned to use manual tools and manual machines; how to weld, solder, and design a robot; how to pick components and materials; how to fundraise; how to work on a long-term project with a team of people; and how to run my own team.

Being on the robotics team solidified my love of engineering and robotics. It was also how I knew I wanted to go to engineering school. When I was applying for colleges, my college counselor suggested I look at an engineering school in Massachusetts called Worcester Polytechnic Institute because WPI had a reputation for being welcoming to women. I applied and was accepted, and I also received a scholarship, which made it possible for me to afford the school.

When I started at WPI, they had just established the first undergraduate degree in robotics engineering in the country. I went on to graduate with a bachelor's degree and a master's degree, both in robotics engineering. My brother also attended WPI, and we both finished our master's degrees at the same time and graduated together. It was a special moment for us.

Even though I didn't become an actress, my mom was right about my big personality, and I have channeled that part of me into entrepreneurship. After finishing my master's degree, I started a robotics company with my dad, where we help schools to start robotics and engineering programs. I also consult with companies on how they can incorporate robotics and automation into their businesses. My goal has always been to develop my own commercial robotics system, and I am happy to say that my brother and I recently founded a new company to do just that.

I am constantly learning and evolving. When I founded my company after graduation, I thought that it would flourish in one particular way, but it didn't. Still, I have continued to work toward that dream, and have made space for new dreams—like becoming an author. I wrote this book for girls to see that even if they have figured out what they want and know who they are, there will still be bumps in the road.

My hope is that *STEAM Powered Girls* helps you to see how special and brilliant you are and that you have so much potential. The only thing you need to tap in to your potential is faith in yourself, your abilities, and your imagination.

INTRODUCTION

This book was written with you in mind, and it is no accident that you are reading it now. *STEAM Powered Girls* is not your ordinary boring book designed to get you to like science, technology, engineering, the arts, and math. If you are attending school or go to an after-school program, people are already telling you how important STEM and STEAM are to your future. With this book we want to empower you to use the many tools of STEAM to get you through this time in your life and help you have a great time as you go through all the crazy things that you have to deal with.

You may not realize it yet, but every aspect of STEAM can be used to come up with a solution to most of the challenges you face, from making big decisions, like where to go to school, who to date, who not to date, when to stand up for something, and when to let something pass, to small things, like deciding what to wear or how to do your hair. We have gone through these challenges, and now we want to show you how to empower yourself to become who you want to be.

A partial list of challenges that you may be facing include the following:

* Your body is changing every day.
* Your parents don't always understand you; they try, but they are so much older, and things are different these days.
* Some days you don't feel pretty.
* You get picked on by others.
* Boys are a mystery.
* You are overwhelmed by all of the options for what you can be.
* There is a lot of competition to get into college.
* Your hormones drive you crazy every month.
* Every time you get used to one technology, another one comes along.
* Trying to keep up on social media can be exhausting and depressing.

The good news is, as a STEAM-powered girl, you will know how to find solutions to these challenges and more. As you read through the book, you will learn the following:

* You are not alone in facing your challenges.
* You are unique, and that uniqueness will serve you if you let it.
* If you choose to see something as bad, it will color everything you do in a negative way.
* Don't worry about what other people say about you, your past, or your future.
* Everybody has an opinion about everything; it doesn't mean that what they say is true for you.
* Don't get addicted to worrying or being concerned about what other people think, especially on social media.

❋   There is always going to be someone who does not like you, your hairstyle, your clothes, or something else about you.

❋   Nobody is everybody's cup of tea.

Challenges serve you, depending on how you look at them. If you see challenges as opportunities for you to show up in all of your infinite amazingness, then you will always be on top. Challenges come into our lives to help us grow. Think about the strong women you know in your life. They also faced many challenges to get where they are today, and each challenge they faced and conquered made them stronger.

To help us understand the challenges today's girls face, we interviewed several girls your age. We asked them what bothers them, what they are nervous about, and what questions they had about getting through middle school and high school. Most importantly, they shared their ideas and dreams about the future. These girls came from many different backgrounds and neighborhoods. Their families had different levels of education and financial resources. We learned that it didn't matter how much money their families had or where they lived; they still shared many of the same concerns. Their responses gave us insights about what is important to girls your age today. While the rapid change in technology creates a variety of challenges in today's world, most of the things these girls were nervous about were the same things their mothers and grandmothers faced.

We also interviewed many STEAM-powered professional women for this book. They spoke about having dealt with many of the same issues that today's girls are facing. We asked them how they faced these challenges, and each woman emphasized that she used her STEAM-powered skills to overcome her challenges and grow stronger. (To read more about each of these incredible and accomplished women, please see appendix A, "Meet Our STEAM-Powered Women.") We, Nola and Lizzy, also dealt with these same issues, and we will share some of our stories with you throughout the chapters, as well.

You will meet sisters Jennifer, who is in high school, and Sara, who is in middle school. Jennifer and Sara will step in here and there throughout the book to give you their perspectives and tell stories you can relate to in order to show you how STEAM-powered girls deal with challenges and make stuff happen.

The only difference between you and the women and girls you will read about in this book is that you have access to brand-new STEAM-powered tools that they didn't have. You will be able to recognize certain types of situations and see them for what they are, like being bullied, feeling like you don't have what it takes to be successful, and figuring out boys. You will be more prepared to handle these daily challenges using your newly developed STEAM power.

One of the most important things you can do on your journey to becoming a STEAM-powered girl is to keep a journal dedicated to your pursuits and interests. You will also use this journal to write down your answers to the exercises found throughout the book. Find a notebook or journal right now to use as you read. Keep it handy every time you open this book so that you can jot down ideas, questions, thoughts, and inspirations.

Finally, we suggest that you re-read the chapters that speak more loudly to you. Mark up your book with a highlighter or pen, and make notes in the margins. Make this book *yours*.

Read this book knowing that it was written with you in mind. The future is bright, and you have the potential to succeed in whatever you do—even when some of your endeavors fail. You have what it takes to get through this time in your life with flying colors. You are the future of our local and global community, and the future looks bright.

All our best to you and your future,
Lizzy and Nola

CHAPTER 1
BEING A TEENAGE GIRL IN TODAY'S WORLD

You can't be perfect all of the time.

– CAROLINA DE LA HORRA

Being a teenager is hard. Period. It's hard for everyone, even for people who make it look easy. Throw in having a changing body, feeling insecure, and being pressured on social media in today's changing world, and you have a perfect brew for everyday life to be challenging. The good news is that you are holding in your hands the secret to becoming a STEAM-powered girl, and STEAM-powered girls have the superpower of being able to use the principles of science, technology, engineering, the arts, and mathematics to solve even the most challenging of problems.

Everyone who has ever accomplished anything worthwhile has faced challenges, but they did not let those challenges stop them or define them. In fact, they used those challenges to create opportunities to support their passions and the great things they went on to accomplish.

Lindsay Bartholomew creates exhibits and develops visitor experiences at the MIT Museum at the Massachusetts Institute of Technology. She says, "I was born with only one finger on each hand, which might make anyone assume that I dealt with bullies a lot. However, I had a core group of friends whom I had met in first grade, and I was in the same school with these friends through eighth grade. They are still my closest friends today. Of course, I always see the second glances that people throw my way, and I always have to field the questions of why and what happened. I tried to look at it from the perspective of others, and I realized that I'd be curious, too. As long as questions came from a place of innocent curiosity or concern, I was OK with them. I think that people see pretty quickly that my physical difference makes no difference to me, and therefore it usually makes no difference to them." Whatever the differences you see or perceive in yourself, if you don't let them bother you and embrace them instead, other people will follow suit, and your differences won't matter to them, either.

Sisters Sara and Jennifer are both learning to turn challenges into opportunities by using STEAM principles. Jennifer is a high school student going through the ups and downs of all that comes with being in high school and being a girl, and Sara is a middle school girl who is facing challenges that she never expected when she was still an elementary school student. The sisters will share their thoughts and stories with you throughout the book, showing you how to use the tools of STEAM to feel strong by being yourself and following your passions, ideas, and dreams.

▶▶▶   Hi, I'm Sara. I'm in middle school. My hobbies are reading, dancing, and playing the piano. I love hanging out with our dog, Marley, and my gerbil, Henry. I have often wondered, what does all this talk about STEM, and now STEAM (they added art), have to do with me? I know it's the popular word for education today, but I don't think it really affects me and the life I'm living right now. School is only a part of my life, and while it may be important to my future, it doesn't impact my everyday life. Or does it? You see, I'm really interested in engineering and robotics, and other science stuff like biology. I don't know a lot about any of those things yet, but I'm inspired to learn more. ◀◀◀

▶▶▶   *Hello, Jennifer here. I'm in high school. I get it; STEAM relates to school work, and if I want to do well in the world and want my future to be bright, I have to do well in those subjects. But at my age, it's only one of the important things going on in my life. Most adults don't understand; I think they forget what it's like to be young.*

That being said, I have loved drawing mechanical things for as long as I can remember. When I was six years old, my dad took our vacuum cleaner apart. I was so fascinated by all the stuff going on inside that I grabbed a pencil and drew the whole inside of the vacuum cleaner. I've been drawing that kind of stuff ever since. I'm really interested in mechanical drawing, so I take a lot of art classes. But I also have to study mechanical engineering so that I understand everything I'm drawing.

I'm really happy to be here to help you understand how to use the principles of STEAM in your everyday life so that you, too, can be an awesome STEAM-powered girl! ◀◀◀

Have you, like Sara, been wondering why you should learn anything about STEAM? That is totally understandable. At your age there are so many things going on in your life, and it hardly seems like STEAM can make a difference. But just as Sara and Jennifer are discovering, these subjects will impact your life and your future far more than you realize.

Always expect bumps and challenges along the way, but if you work hard and are persistent, then you will eventually succeed.
– DEBRA ENGLANDER

Throughout your life you will be faced with many challenges. (If you think you have a lot of challenges now, just wait.) But here's the thing: the more challenges you have before you, the more power you have over your life.

Let's look at some common challenges you may be facing right now. All of these issues are what girls have been dealing with for centuries, with the exception of social media challenges; that's pretty new. The good news is that today you have new tools to use to get you through and to not only survive these years but thrive.

Do you relate to any of the following challenges? All of them? That's normal! Let's take a look.

FEELING AWKWARD

Everyone feels awkward sometime or another.
– ELIZABETH TURNER

Everyone feels awkward sometimes, and everyone has insecurities. Growing up and doing things that are new and that make you feel uncomfortable is part of that. Everyone is awkward when they are doing or learning something new. In fact, one of the things adults remember most about being in middle school is feeling awkward. It is a theme that all of the women we interviewed specifically mentioned. Mechanical engineer Lisa Winter says, "I felt awkward the majority of the time because of how shy I was. I tried to deal with this by forming my thoughts in my head first before speaking."

Middle school is an age when you are transitioning from being a little kid to being a teenager. You experience a lot of physical changes, and your parents, teachers, and friends also have changing expectations of you. Transition times are always hard, and you are trying to learn what you like, what you are good at, and most importantly, who you are.

Middle school is the epitome of awkward and uncomfortable because so many things are changing so fast, and you're just trying to keep up.
– ANGELINE GROSS

Middle school girls often look up to high school girls. High school girls are older, so they will often have relevant advice, but it is important to remember that it is not advice from an adult. Lisa Winter notes: "Three factors are necessary for advice to be successful: timing, location, and acceptance. These three factors need to be present for advice to be relevant and useful. The person getting the advice needs to be in the right place and time in their life to use the advice. They also need to be open to accepting the advice. I've heard lots of advice over the years, and sometimes it doesn't soak in until the second or third time I hear it. My advice is to listen and keep an open mind, since you never know what seemingly small piece of information will be useful at some point in life."

Lizzy here. You also want to be careful with your own words of advice for the same reason. When I was in high school, we would go on a retreat with our entire grade every year. A retreat is when you step away from your day-to-day responsibilities and use the time to pray, reflect, meditate, and learn about yourself.

When I was a sophomore, our class retreat was two days long. On the night of the first day the whole class did a large-group exercise. Before the retreat, we wrote letters to other girls in our class and told them about a moment when they made an impact on us. Then we read them out loud at the retreat, and talked about those moments we were thankful for. One of the girls sent me a letter that told about a time when she was having a really bad day. She wrote that I saw her in the hallway, smiled at her, and said something nice. She wrote how important and impactful my action was, and she was thankful because it really made a difference to her. I was struck by her message at the retreat because I don't remember the day she was talking about or what I said to her. But that moment taught me that we can make a difference without even realizing it. Every small act we do can make a real difference, and we decide and control the kind of impact we want to make on the world and the people around us.

◀◀◀▶▶▶

Surgeon Michele Loor says, "Everyone feels like an outsider at some point. This happens not just in middle school but throughout life. I have attended meetings where I questioned whether I should be participating, and I have been in social circles where I didn't feel comfortable. In these cases, I think it is important to figure out what is meaningful for you, and veer away from doing those things that are not. Remember who you are and what you believe in, and let that guide you through uncomfortable situations."

Software engineer Julia Cherushevich notes that there are different types of uncomfortable feelings. One is being uncomfortable because you are pushing yourself and growing, which is "good" discomfort. The other is being uncomfortable because the situation you are in or the people around you are bad for your well-being. Sometimes it's hard to differentiate between the two when you are in middle school.

The most important thing is to be a good person and be nice to others, even when you feel awkward.

Feeling Insecure

One of the common things everyone struggles with in middle and high school is insecurity. Insecurity about your looks, speaking in front of the classroom (also known as public speaking), and what your classmates think of you are a part of life. You may worry about being cool, but you really just want to feel accepted and have people like you. This is completely normal. Wanting to feel accepted for who you are and liked by your peers is not just a part of school but a part of life. Many adults deal with the same feelings. However, the way to find friends and loved ones who truly accept you and like you for yourself is to learn how to love, respect, and accept yourself first.

Dentist-turned-entrepreneur and designer Amanda Davila knows well the feeling of insecurity. She says, "My experience as a middle school girl was interesting. I studied hard, got good grades, was part of the cheerleading team, and excelled at sports, but I always had a hard time making friends. I liked drawing and coloring, singing and dancing, and felt my best when I was doing these things, but I was usually by myself since I was so shy.

"I didn't want anybody—especially my classmates—to find out about my drawings, so I would hide them. However, one day the arts teacher saw them and thought it would be a good idea for me to sign up for a national arts competition. I remember feeling my stomach turn upside down at the mere thought of standing in front of judges and showing them one of my illustrations. How could I do that? In front of everybody? No way! I thought the challenge was bigger than I could handle, but my parents encouraged me, so I did it. I felt very scared the day I had to present my drawing, but I won second place! I received a prize and an award ribbon. If I had let my fear and insecurity take the best of me, I would have never found out that other people liked my drawings."

Xyla Foxlin, a mechatronics engineer and executive director of her own nonprofit, also knows the fear of insecurity. She says, "Freshman year of college I was alone in the robotics lab at three o'clock in the morning, on the brink of a meltdown. My design wasn't coming together because I had made a mistake in fabrication, but our team was headed to NASA for a competition in just a few days, and I had to make it work. A graduate student who shared the lab with us wandered in and saw me struggling. Instead of helping me solve the problem or do it for me, he said, 'You played violin growing up, didn't you? How many hours did you pour into playing that instrument? Engineering is no different: it's an art, and it takes practice. You just started this year; you're basically still learning your scales. Don't be so hard on yourself.' Don't be so hard on yourself! It isn't about just knowing something; you need to put in the time."

Lizzy here. I, too, have felt insecure. I studied engineering, and to graduate I had to do a senior design project, or "Masters Qualifying Project," as it was called. I was on a team of five people, and we worked all year on the project. At the end of the project we had to do a big presentation in front of all my classmates and professors. I was really nervous and worried what my classmates would think of me and my work.

My thoughts started to race. Sometimes when something gets in my head, it becomes all I can focus on. I stop breathing, my mouth becomes dry, and it's like I am in another world, where the only things I can hear and see are my thoughts. What will my professors think? Will I fail this project? Will I be able to graduate? What will my classmates think? Will they finally realize how stupid I am? Will they see how unprepared I am? Will my professors be disappointed in me? Suddenly my team was called, and it was our turn to give our presentation. There was no turning back.

The presentation was going well, but when it was my turn, I started panicking: my heart racing, everything closing in, the room closing in, everyone's eyes on me, staring into me like they could see every problem, every thought, every insecurity. I saw a friend of mine sitting in the last row, laughing. I thought he was laughing at me, and I got so upset that I skipped a slide and didn't finish my presentation.

I left the presentation crying, thinking I had completely failed my project. I didn't want to leave my room after that, but two days later I found that I got a B on the project. I had lunch with my friend who had been laughing, and out of nowhere he asked me, "Why did you skip a slide in your presentation?" I was still upset about it, so I was honest and said, "I panicked and thought you all in the back were laughing at me." He looked at me and said, "I'm so sorry. I feel so bad about that, but the guy next to me had made a random joke and I thought it was funny. It had nothing to do with your presentation."

This was when I realized how hard we can be on ourselves. We don't know what other people are thinking, and we can't assume that they are thinking the worst about us. The best way to ensure that we don't get upset by what other people might think about us is to focus on what we think about ourselves. If I had focused on being confident about all of my hard work and all that I had learned over the course of the year, I would have realized that I should be proud to share that with my friends. Obviously, I knew more than they did about my project because I had spent a whole year working on it, and the reason they had gone to my presentation was because they wanted to support me.

◀◀◆▶▶

You will sometimes hear the phrase "fake it 'til you make it," but we think it's better as "*face* it 'til you make it." When you work every day to face the things that scare you and are hard, then every day you will get a little stronger, until one day you conquer them.

Human resources professional Patricia Fors suggests that when you feel insecure about something, ask yourself if you will care about it in six months or a year from now, then ask yourself if you still care about stuff that happened last year. This helps put things into perspective and is an exercise that serves as a good mental check-in. It can be tough to put your insecurities into perspective, but the only way to get past them and feel liked and accepted is to focus on liking and accepting who you are.

Things happen in life, and you can either laugh
about them or cry about them. But laughing
about them always feels much better.
– ELIZABETH DE ZULUETA

Feeling insecure about yourself as a teenage girl is normal, common, and temporary. As you develop your STEAM powers, your confidence and belief in yourself will grow and grow throughout your school years. Keep reminding yourself that things change, that you are maturing, and that you are developing the superpower of being a STEAM-powered girl.

When you feel the need to tap in to your STEAM-powered superpowers, try doing a power pose. We like to call it the Wonder Woman pose. Stand tall, legs straight, feet a little wider than hip width apart, with your chest up and your hands on your hips. Hold this pose for one to three minutes as you breathe deeply and visualize what you want to accomplish. For instance, if you are going to give a presentation, do the Wonder Woman pose just before you go before your audience, and visualize doing really well on your presentation. This will help you to feel calmer and more confident. You can even do it in the bathroom before a test.

WANTING TO BE ACCEPTED OR POPULAR

Fitting in is about assessing a situation and becoming who you need to be to be accepted. Belonging, on the other hand, doesn't require us to change who we are; it requires us to be who we are.
– BRENÉ BROWN

Everyone wants to be accepted into a group. Humans are social beings who have a need to be accepted and loved. Even animals like dogs and cats want to be loved and accepted by their owners. Our families love us and accept us, even though they might have different ideas of what we should or should not be doing. Our friends and others around us can have an effect on us as we try to fit in and get their approval. We all want to be liked and accepted, and there's nothing wrong with that.

Cardiologist Ana Victoria Soto-Quintela remembers, "I had a clique of female friends, but when I succeeded in school, I was kicked out of their group. This was hurtful, and as I grew up, it shaped my opinion of females in general and how I should behave in an academic setting. After that experience I made new friends, but I held back at times during class in order to not seem too smart or know all the answers. As a result, making long-lasting female relationships was a big challenge. The fields of medicine and cardiology are male-dominated, so I felt comfortable making friends with my male colleagues during my residency and fellowship, as men were more to the point, used less subliminal messaging, and were open about their feelings. I eventually came to have great female friends, but they were few and far between. Because of that early experience, middle school shaped me far beyond those years."

It is important to work hard to understand how awesome and special you are and that there is never going to be another you, ever, in the whole world. There are times when you might forget how unique you are and look outside of yourself to get approval. The problem comes when we change who we are in order to be accepted, but then we are not accepted, no matter how hard we try to conform. Also, selling yourself out eventually comes back to hurt you. Besides, the people you are trying to impress to get their approval will no longer be in your life down the road. Ask any adult you know if they remember all the people in their lives whom they tried to impress, and if it was worth it.

Singer-songwriter Jackie Garcia de Quevedo says, "I felt uncomfortable and awkward around the popular group of girls in school. I would try to fit in, and I never allowed myself to be myself out of fear they wouldn't like me. I remember several occasions when I was not true to myself so that I could fit in. At those moments I never felt less uncomfortable, and in fact I felt more alone."

Setting good priorities can help build confidence and lead you down the best path. Rachel Winsten, who works in the field of environmental health and safety, says, "Growing up, I often felt awkward and uncomfortable in social situations. As I grew older, I realized where my priorities lay and that popularity in school wouldn't matter later in life. This perspective helped me gain confidence. I was able to go into college self-assured and confident in myself and my abilities. Now, when I feel awkward or uncomfortable, I push myself to face the situation. If I fail or embarrass myself, I take it as a learning experience and look for ways I can improve for the future."

You will always be hardest on yourself, but what you may not realize is that the people around you are not judging you as much as you think they are.

Lizzy here. I am one of those people who had to learn this lesson many times before it stuck. When I was in seventh grade, I went to a school that had a conservatory. I wanted to take dance classes like all the cool girls, but my parents couldn't afford them. Luckily, my dad knew a martial arts instructor who was willing to allow my brother and me to take classes at his school in return for help with his computer.

I loved and excelled at my martial arts classes. Not only did our instructor teach us to defend ourselves and be physically strong, he also taught us life lessons and focused on making his students mentally and emotionally strong. My brother and I practiced often and took notes after every class, so we developed our skills very quickly.

I never told my classmates that I took martial arts classes after school, but one day my dad told my after-school teacher, and she thought it would be fun if we gave a demonstration for everyone. I wasn't sure, but my teacher wanted me to do it, so I didn't want to say no.

I constantly get stuck in my head, and when I am nervous, my thoughts start racing. What will my friends think? Will they think it is stupid or weird? Will they think I am ugly or not girly? Will they judge me? But I had already agreed to do the demonstration, my dad was already at the school with my equipment, I had already changed into my martial arts uniform, and the teacher had already told the other students I was going to show them what I had learned in my martial arts class. There was no turning back.

I started with a few basic punching drills, which I had done a million times and knew I could do even if I was nervous. Then my dad and I took out our Kali sticks. Filipino Kali is a martial art from the Philippines that uses hard rattan sticks to strike and defend. I loved my Kali class; it was and still is one of my favorite styles of martial arts.

My dad and I did some basic stick combinations and drills. Watching someone practice Kali can be intimidating because the sticks make a loud noise when they hit each other. I had practiced often, so I could execute some of the most basic drills very fast.

Since I love Kali and was focused on what I was doing instead of having all those thoughts running through my head, I was able to finish my demonstration. Everyone was quiet for several seconds, but then the whole class started to clap. After the demonstration, a few students approached me to tell me how cool it was and that they were really impressed. I was proud of myself for having done the demonstration, and none of the horrible thoughts I had running through my head turned out to be true. My friends and classmates didn't judge me for any activity I loved and excelled at.

◀◀◇▶▶

Lizzy's experience served as a lesson that you cannot assume what your peers are thinking about you. We usually assume they are thinking the worst, although that is not often the case. Wanting to be liked is a feeling that never goes away; we all deal with it throughout our lives.

Being in Middle School

I loved middle school. Math, art, and science classes were all super fun, and the many hands-on projects made learning even more fun.
– LISA WINTER

Middle school was probably the worst two years of my life.
– XYLA FOXLIN

Being in middle school is sometimes great and sometimes hard. So many things are different. Life in elementary school was so simple. Most of the kids were fun and friendly, the schoolwork was easy, and the teachers were always there to help. One of the mistakes we make is not being present in the moment; we wish we were somewhere else and in some other time. We think that the present needs to speed up so we can get on to better things.

Sometimes that is understandable. Xyla Foxlin says, "I moved to a new school district and had come from a background that was much different from that of my new peers. They were much wealthier and had private tutors, their own iPod Touches (I'm dating myself here!), and their own computers. I didn't even know how to type or use Google. I had gone to elementary school in a diverse town full of immigrants and working-class families. We played outside after school and made crafts out of found items; we didn't take extra math classes or play on the computer. I went from being at the top of my class and winning all the engineering activities to struggling in this new district's classes. My love of math, science, and building things completely disappeared, and I started scribbling "No Math Zone" and "I hate math" on the front of my notebooks. I struggled to make new friends, and was bullied so much that the neighbor who lived in the house overlooking the school bus stop told my parents to start driving me to school."

Lisa Roberts, who works as a medical coder, says, "When I was in middle school, I won the position of president of the pep club. My sister was five years older and in high school. I had seen what their pep club did to promote school spirit, so I had many good ideas to raise money and sell fun items to promote our school spirit. When the principal found out that I had been voted as president, she dissolved the club; I believe she did it because I had a behavior problem in school. I was in trouble for some of my earlier actions, and I believe that the principal didn't want me to have any kind of recognition. I was very disappointed when she cancelled the club, but I had definitely had that coming to me as a result of my behavior. The funny thing was that I was so happy and felt so good about myself for winning that election."

School is just a vehicle to achieve one's goals.
– ALINA TRUEBA

One of the most difficult parts about middle school is feeling like something embarrassing could happen in front of your friends, classmates, crushes, or teachers. Another is the idea that if you do something wrong or embarrassing, everyone will remember it forever. The thing is, embarrassing things will happen, but they won't last forever. People will forget, and eventually you will either forget it happened or remember it as a funny story.

Lizzy here. We wore uniforms in my middle school, and the girls' uniform had a skirt. I liked a boy in my class named Dennis. One day after school, some of my classmates and I were playing tag, and I asked Dennis if he wanted to play. Right when I was talking to him, a gust of wind came by, blew the front of my skirt up over my face, and he saw my underwear. I was so embarrassed I didn't know what to do, so I just turned and ran. I thought everyone had noticed and that they would make fun of me the next day. But nothing happened! No one ever mentioned it, and I was eventually able to laugh over it. Was it really embarrassing? Yes! Those things happen, but you shouldn't be scared that they will define you.

◄◄◄►►►

You cannot always control what happens, but you can control how you react to it. So, if you ever get hit by a gust of wind and have your skirt blown into your face, just fix it, laugh, and continue playing with your friends.

FEELING OVERWHELMED

Anybody can wrestle a bear for a little while.
– CATHI COX-BONIOL

Overwhelm is the feeling of being overpowered by life situations. In all phases of our lives we can feel overwhelmed for any number of reasons and from many different directions. It can come as a result of pressure to succeed at school, work on a project, meet a time deadline, live up to family expectations, act a certain way, or like or dislike something or someone. Overwhelm can also come from overcommitting ourselves and not feeling like we have enough time to complete everything. It can even come from trying to please everyone else and not being true to ourselves.

The feeling of being overwhelmed can have physical reactions in the body, such as shortness of breath, heart palpitations, and nausea. We can also have emotional reactions, like feeling we are going to start crying uncontrollably.

The only person who can control your reactions to overwhelm is you. Yes, as with almost all other situations, you are totally in control of how you respond. Sometimes you might wish that you could turn to someone else and have them turn off the whole thing with a word or action, but in reality, only you are in control of your reactions. While we cannot control what happens to us or around us, we can control how we react and how we are affected afterward.

Fearing Failure

Fear is unknown baggage.
– RAMONITA MARTINEZ

One thing that people of all ages face is the fear of failing: failing an important test, failing to make the team, or failing whatever it is that is important to you. There are times when just the fear of failing itself makes failure happen. Everyone fears failing at different things, but this fear does not need to take over your life.

When you are afraid of failing something, the best thing to do is to recognize whatever it is that makes you feel uneasy and remember that you are not alone. Sometimes just remembering that fact helps to make a situation not feel so bad. Thinking that you are the only one who feels a certain way is scary. Remembering that feeling fearful is normal often takes the sting out of the fear—at least, enough to move through it and bring your strong self forward.

Monica De Zulueta, a technical strategist for Microsoft, points out, "Every failure is a learning experience. You remember your failures more vividly than your successes. When you stumble and have to work through a challenge, the experience of learning how to resolve it and then doing so will always teach you more and stay with you longer than if you had done it right the first time."

Take risks even if it means failing.
That is the only way to become better at anything.
– ANA VICTORIA SOTO-QUINTELA

Worrying about Your Looks

I went through a lot of physical changes in my middle school years, but sometimes I felt like I wasn't changing enough. I felt I wasn't good enough, and I kept comparing myself to the other girls.
– JACKIE GARCIA DE QUEVEDO

We might admit it only to ourselves, but worrying about the way we look is something that can feel strong and silly at the same time. Many of the girls we interviewed quietly admitted that they worry about their looks: I think I'm too fat; my boobs aren't growing in as fast as my friends'; my hair is too curly, too straight, too frizzy; I'm too skinny; my butt looks too big (or too small); my eyes aren't the right color; my skin is too light (or too dark); and on and on.

We asked the girls we talked with to give their description of the "perfect girl" and were amazed that most of the girls described someone who did not look anything like themselves. Across the board, girls are mostly not comfortable with their looks. Predictably, there were many, many different descriptions of the perfect girl. What does that mean? It means that what you look like fits at least one person's description of the perfect girl: dark hair with dark eyes, dark hair with light eyes, thin with curly hair, thin with straight hair, heavier with straight hair and dark eyes, heavier with curly hair and light eyes. You name it, some combination of all of the physical attributes we have is someone's vision of the perfect girl. However you look, whatever combination of attributes you have been blessed with, celebrate them!

Not Understanding Boys

We admit it: teenage boys are a mystery. If you expect boys to think and act like girls, you're being naïve and not taking many things into account! Think about the difference between cats and monkeys: you would never expect a cat to act or run or play like a monkey, and you will never see a monkey purr and curl up in your lap like a cat. Like cats and monkeys, males and females are two different kinds of human beings with biologically different brains, different hormones running through their bodies, and different anatomies.

Teen girls talk about boys a lot. This is the time when you start to develop crushes and begin to worry about what boys are thinking. You might be told to stay away from them or not think about them at all. But the thing is, interacting with boys, just like interacting with all of your peers, will always be a part of life.

One of the hardest things to figure out is what boys are thinking because of how they talk to you. Your male classmates, friends, or crushes might make fun of you and then not understand why you are mad. Remember, both boys and girls have insecurities and want to be liked by their classmates and their crushes, but boys and girls communicate and bond very differently.

When one of your girlfriends is upset, you support her by telling her how awesome she is and pointing out what she is good at, maybe even by comparing it to something you are bad at. For instance, your friend is crying because she made a mistake at her dance recital. To support her, you tell her she is an amazing dancer and that you wish you could dance as well as she does. Girls and women do this because we want our girlfriends to know how much we admire their talents, that they have talents that other people do not, and that they should be proud of their talents.

Please note that putting yourself down is not the best answer when trying to cheer up a friend, but it is something girls and women do when we bond and talk to each other. Boys communicate and bond in the opposite way. They get together and tease each other. Boys focus on what they themselves are good at and joke about what their friends are not good at.

Noticing that you might be developing crushes or feelings for your classmates or friends can be overwhelming and intimidating. What do they think of me? Do they like me? What kinds of girls do they like? All of these questions can seem like a big deal, but the reality is, the boys are going through the same thought processes. They are suddenly realizing that they might have crushes and are wondering what girls think about them, too! Regardless of whether a boy is a crush or just a friend, the important thing to remember is that people like and want to be around people who like and accept themselves.

FACING BODY CHANGES AND HORMONES

*One can feel self-conscious because of body changes,
and that leads to not putting oneself out there, taking
new opportunities, and having confidence in one's abilities.*
– ELIZABETH TURNER

Up until now your body has been pretty manageable. You have been the same from the time you can remember, with a few exceptions: teeth falling out and bigger teeth take their place, and clothes and shoes get smaller. Basically, though, you have just grown taller and bigger. All of a sudden that's not true anymore, and big changes have snuck up on you out of the blue. You feel moody for no apparent reason, cry over silly stuff and big stuff, get your period, grow hair in places where there was none before, and your breasts get bigger. These changes can be unsettling if you're not ready for them, and even if you learned about them, it's not the same as experiencing them.

Attorney Elizabeth Turner says, "Middle school was very rough for me. I started at a new school in sixth grade and was one of only six new kids. It was really hard to fit in with people who had been together since kindergarten. On top of that, I seemed to go through reverse puberty: I was a thin kid until sixth grade, and then I gained weight. Middle school is such a formative time for young girls, and being chubby made me afraid to put myself out there. I was always successful academically, so I spent a lot of time focusing on my studies. A lot of my problems centered on my weight. One time, I was shopping with a friend and was helping her look for jeans. The store clerk came up to me and said, "We don't carry your size here." That memory is seared into my brain. I got upset and left, but I didn't cry. It was the first time (but not the last) that someone said something like that to my face. It made me realize that people will say ugly things, but as long as I didn't think those ugly thoughts, it didn't matter."

We give words their power and meaning. If we don't give other people's words meaning, then those words are literally meaningless.

Patricia Fors clearly remembers her changing body. "Middle school was definitely the most awkward period of my existence. I had braces, and one time I cut my own bangs, which was . . . not a good look. I also struggled with envy. I thought all of my friends were prettier than me, and skinner than me, and more developed than me. I was envious of girls who developed more quickly than I did. Those girls were called hot, while I was referred to as cute, which I absolutely hated.

"I have looked young for my age my whole life. I didn't start my period until high school, and I was flat-chested until college. I also thought I was chubby. Now, when I look back at the pictures from that time in my life, I can see how insane my thinking was. I was so uncomfortable in my own skin, and I regret how much time and energy I wasted agonizing about how I looked instead of just enjoying myself. I wish I had smiled broadly in my school photos instead of doing an awkward closed smile over my braces.

When you get to the point where there is too much to do and everyone is expecting too much from you, you would be smart to stop doing everything and take a break. Go for a walk and get a change of scenery. Take some deep breaths outside, and listen for signs of nature. Move every part of your body to get the blood flowing to every cell, including your brain. In your journal, make a list of at least five things that make you feel happy. It could be your pet, a song, or a memory. It shouldn't be hard to think of five things that bring you joy.

Take at least fifteen minutes to enjoy getting away from all of your to-do's. After you're done, sit down and make a list of all the things you need to do. Then put a number in front of each item in order of importance. How many of them do you *have* to get done today? You can only do one thing at a time really well, so on the back of the list, write down the most important item, and just do that one thing. When you're finished, draw a line through it. Then take a five-minute break, even if it is only to look out the window. Take some deep breaths, and think of at least three things that make you happy.

Now go back to your list and write down on the back of the paper the next most important thing on your list, and do that one. You get the idea. Life is more manageable if we take it one thing at a time. Every time you complete something, you will be more empowered and feel more successful.

Being Overwhelmed by Social Media

Never post something that may haunt you later.
– DOTTIE FAUERBACH

Today you face a challenge that none of the women who came before you had, which is having to deal with social media, such as Facebook,

Instagram, Twitter, YouTube, and TikTok. Trying to keep up with what is going on in your friends' lives through their posts can be daunting. You see the pictures they post, activities they participate in, and the everyday lives they seem to be living. Sometimes it looks like they have perfect lives, that they don't have any problems, that they have it all. But that is not necessarily their true reality.

When people try to make others think that they don't have any challenges to deal with, they are not being truthful about their real lives. As long as you are alive you will have challenges to deal with, and so will they. Everyone deals with family problems; parents who do not understand their kids; school; health stuff; and relationships with friends, boys, teachers, and bosses. Don't be fooled by what people post. Be happy for the good things that happen to others and count your own blessings, but do not believe that what you see posted on social media is the whole truth, or that you have to measure up to it.

Do any of the challenges we discussed in this chapter feel familiar to you? They're pretty common with teenage girls.

Many things will happen in your life that you cannot control, and some things might even rock you to the core. There will be times that you feel like you can't control your life anymore and that everything is new and scary. You will just want things to go back to the way they were. Whether changes happen as a result of losing a loved one, a friend moving away, moving to a new school, a pandemic, or any number of reasons that change happens, you will get through it, day by day. You will discover you are stronger, more resilient, and more resourceful than you think.

As a STEAM-powered girl, you are going to have tools and strategies for dealing with all of the problems we discussed in this chapter and more, and you will be able to use them for the rest of your life. In the next chapter, you will learn what the STEAM principles are and how they apply to real life.

CHAPTER 2

The Principles of STEAM

*Technology is a tool. The goal is to make
harder things easier, not easy things harder.*

– MONICA DE ZULUETA

As you become familiar with and learn to apply the tools and principles of STEAM, others will start to notice you as a girl who stands out not because of the clothes you wear—although you can be a fashion diva if you choose—but for your ability to find solutions to life's everyday challenges.

The principles behind using science, technology, engineering, the arts, and mathematics are important to understand so that you can apply them to life's challenges. In this chapter we will explore exactly what STEAM is, and then we'll talk about some of the most important STEAM principles you will learn to solve problems and address challenges.

Wʜᴀᴛ Is STEAM?

The real heart of STEAM is thinking
creatively to solve a problem.
– ANGELINE GROSS

Simply put, STEAM stands for science, technology, engineering, the arts, and mathematics. Just so you're clear, we're going to define each of these fields for you.

The common use of the word "steam" refers to the gas created when water is heated, but here we are using it as an acronym to mean a combination of subjects, careers, and methods of creating. Each subject in STEAM is an important one, and each will help you to develop several different skills to help you accomplish the goals you set for yourself. Our goal through this book is to show you that, just like steam was used to power ships and trains and many other machines, you can use STEAM to empower yourself and use that power to accomplish any goal and overcome any obstacle.

The concept of STEAM education and STEAM principles were developed by educator and researcher Georgette Yakman and were later expanded and made popular by the Rhode Island School of Design. Their focus was to teach students that critical thinking and creativity are at the core of innovation. They wanted to demonstrate that science, technology, engineering, art, and math work together to influence the world around us. Before we can dive into how all of these different subjects overlap with each other, we'll break them down so you can get a better understand of each one. Then you will see get a clearer picture of how they intertwine.

Science is defined as the careful study of the structure and behavior of the physical world, especially by watching, measuring, and performing experiments. Basically, science is the process of observing the world around you, writing down what you see, and then trying different things to better understand, change, or fix what you observe.

To achieve progress, change is necessary.
– AMY CUTTING

Technology is an expansion of the concepts you learn when studying science. It is defined as the application of scientific knowledge to the practical aim of human life or to change the human environment. Technology includes everything from tools and processes to ideas and products. Anything that uses science or engineering to change how you interact with the world around you is considered technology. This means that any time you make or use something that changes how you interact with your room, house, car, or school, you are making or using technology.

We hear on the news that technology is everywhere now, and this is true. But the reality is, technology has been everywhere for a long time, starting with the first tools made by cavemen to help them skin pelts and prepare food. As humans, we are constantly trying to make our lives better, easier, safer, and more efficient. We do this by using the tools and information we have available: technology.

Engineering is the use of scientific principles to design and build machines, structures, processes, and systems. Engineering is often confused with technology, so you might wonder what the difference is. They are actually interconnected, which is why they seem so similar. But our view as engineers is that technology is what engineers build when they solve a problem people want solved.

Engineers love solving problems; it is how we are trained. However, sometimes we forget that not every solution is the best one to solve the problem; the solution has to help the people experiencing the problem.

The person who uses what we build is called the "user." To make a solution that a user needs, we must talk and listen to that person. We must observe not only the problem but also the user's current method of dealing with it. That way we can build something that is practical and applicable to their life. This is where the slight difference between engineering and technology is found. Engineering is the process of thinking through the problem, designing something, and then building it. Technology is what we build or engineer that solves a problem, has a practical application in the real world, or makes life better or easier for the user.

It may surprise you that we would include *the arts* with science, technology, engineering, and math. Usually we think that building a robot and painting a portrait (or writing a musical) are two very different activities. They are different, there are also many similarities. We often think of the definition of art as the conscious use of skill and creative imagination, especially in the production of aesthetic objects. In other words, we tend to think of art as the use of skills and creativity to make things that are only meant to be looked at or listened to and admired. But the Merriam-Webster dictionary describes art as a skill acquired through experience, study, and observation, and this is where art coincides with the rest of STEAM.

The arts are an essential part of science and engineering because you need skill, experience, study, and observation to successfully apply scientific and mathematical principles in the real world. We tend to forget that a key factor in the sciences is creativity and imagination. All of the scientists, engineers, mathematicians, artists, and musicians you hear and read about spent many nights looking up at the sky and dreaming about what was up there with the stars; or how to build big, cool buildings; or what exotic animals and plants might still be hidden deep in the forest; or how a tree would dance.

To make a new discovery, you have to be willing to look in unexpected places; use creativity to come up with different experiments; and imagine new methods and tools for measuring, observing, and testing. To invent new technologies, you have to be able to imagine gadgets that have never been created before. To invent something in the real world, you first have to dream it in your own world and imagine how it will help someone or make the world a better place. Inventing something new takes consistent, diligent work, just like learning an instrument or a new dance routine does. Learning the scales, how to read music, and how to take care of your instrument may seem like boring tasks, but understanding the importance of these basic skills and implementing them is what makes it possible for your imagination to create new sounds and experiences.

Mathematics is the science of numbers and their operations, interrelations, combinations, generalizations, and abstractions, as well as the study of space configurations and their structures, measurement, transformation, and generalizations. Essentially, math is the study of the physical world through numbers. How numbers work together tells us a lot about how we see and interact with the world. Math can help us understand everything from which furniture to choose based on the dimensions of a room to the spirals on a crab shell to how an apple falls off a tree. Math is the basis of these things because it allows us to break down the world and our experiences into their simplest and most basic versions. When you look at something for the first time in its most basic version, with the least amount of extra information, you can better understand the core of what you are observing. Then, as you gain understanding, you can add in more information or variables to get a fuller picture of what you are analyzing or experiencing.

The five STEAM subjects may all seem quite different from each other when you first study them as separate subjects in school, but the reality is that they all build on one another. When you combine them, you get a deeper and fuller understanding and appreciation of the world and your place in it.

The STEAM framework is a way for all subjects to relate to each other. Science and technology are interpreted through engineering and the arts, and all are based in mathematics.
– GEORGETTE YAKMAN

STEAM Principles of Context and Content

Every action you take has a consequence.
– RAMONITA MARTINEZ

One of the most important principles you can develop as a STEAM-powered girl is to understand and apply the concepts of *context* and *content*, and knowing the important differences between the two. Once you understand these two concepts, you will more easily be able to apply the STEAM principles to solve problems.

As you know, there are times in life when things happen and are just annoying, and then there are times when things happen and hit you hard. You always have a choice of how to react—*always*. Sometimes it is the only control you have over a situation. You may not always have a say in what goes on, but you certainly have 100 percent control over how you look at the situation, how you respond, and how you move forward. This is where knowing the difference between content and context comes in. There is only a one-letter difference between the two words but a world of difference in their meanings.

To illustrate content and context, let's use a painting with a frame around it as a metaphor. Think of the frame as the context and the painting itself as the content. The frame stays the same (context), but the painting can change day by day or minute by minute (content). The term *context* refers to things that, like the frame, generally remain the same: love for your family and friends, your favorite subject in school, your passions in life. The term *content* refers to the things that, like the painting, can change or be changed, like having a fight with your best friend, being annoyed at your mom, or having to take a class you don't like. None of these examples is permanent; they change.

For instance, think about someone you love, like a parent, your pet, or your best friend. The frame of that relationship, the context, is, I love this person (or pet) a lot. The painting inside of the frame, or the content, can change: I'm so mad at my mom; she just grounded me for not getting home on time, or I'm so mad at my dog! He pooped on the carpet in my room. But a few hours later, the content changes: My mom is so cool. She let me explain why I was late, and I'm not grounded after all. In fact, we're going to the movies together tonight, or I love my dog so much; he loves me, too, and he cuddles up with me at night.

Do you see how the day-to-day, even the minute-by-minute, things can change in your life? Most of the situations we encounter are content: the dog pooped on the floor. They happen inside a context, something that is stable and generally stays the same: I love my dog. If you pause to determine whether the situation that is causing concern is related to content or context, it makes it easier to deal with. Most situations are related to content, and it is easier to deal with something that changes often. OK, my dog pooped on the floor. It stinks and is really gross to clean up, but remembering that I still love him makes it not quite so bad.

On the other hand, it would be another story if your brother's friend's dog, whom you do not like at all because he is a rough, snappy dog, came in to your room and pooped on your floor. The context, the thing that remains stable, is, I really don't like that dog; he annoys me every time I see him. The content, the thing that changed, is that now he pooped on the floor in your room. You still have to clean up the poop, most likely moaning and complaining about the guy's dog and the fact that the dog will *never* come into your room again. Cleaning up the poop seems more gross, more stinky, and worse than if your dog had done it. The *context* of your relationship with each dog is different, so your reaction to each one's pooping on your floor is quite different.

Sometimes it takes longer to get over a situation when the context of the relationship is different from what you're used to. Remembering this can help you to realize what is going on inside your head and heart.

▶▶▶   Sara: I finally came to realize that any negative feelings I hold on to don't affect the other person (or dog), but if I carry those feelings around, it can and does affect me. ◀◀◀

Science has proven that the thoughts and feelings we carry around with us, whether positive or negative, impact the trillions of cells in our bodies. The same principle can be applied to two similar situations: you react to each one based on the context of your relationship to the person or situation.

Let's say you're walking down the hall in school, and one of your friends, Suzanne, bumps into you and knocks one of the books in your hands onto the floor. No big deal, right? She apologizes and goes to pick up the book for you. You smile and say, "No problem! I've got it." You move on, and the situation doesn't bother you one bit. The context is that Suzanne is a friend, and the content is that she bumped into you and knocked a book on the floor.

Later that day, you're walking down the hall, and Holly, a girl you can't stand, bumps into you and knocks one of your books onto the floor. It is the same content as with Suzanne (she bumps into you, knocks a book onto the floor), but the context is different (you can't stand her). Holly starts to apologize, but you give her a mean look. She goes to pick up the book, but you push her hand away and snap, "I've got it!" You turn and walk down the hall, thinking how clumsy Holly is and what a pain it was to have to pick up your book. Same scenario (content), but you have different relationships (context) with each of them, so you have two different reactions to the same situation.

Understanding the conceptual difference between context and content can make a big difference in how you choose to react to life's situations. You are in control, so you can decide how to move forward or respond to the situation.

What would happen if you had reacted to Holly the same way you did to Suzanne? Maybe Holly would feel better, which would change her actions for the rest of the day. Maybe she would think that school isn't as crummy a place as she thought. You never know what impact a little thing like that can make on others. You could leave the scene feeling like you did a good deed, and your entire body and all its trillions of cells would get the message that things are good, and it would not have to produce adrenaline to deal with any upset. Your heart and soul would get a positive boost, and you would move forward not feeling grumpy.

The more often you choose to see things as changeable content and not worth getting upset about, the more you will add to the positive growth of yourself and your soul.

Helping others helps you grow.
– STEPHANIE HOLMQUIST

▶▶▶ *Jennifer: Once I could recognize the difference between content and context, dealing with life became a whole lot easier. Now I pick my battles more carefully. Usually, when something happens around me or to me and I recognize it as content, I don't pay as much attention to it. I do my best to lighten up and let it pass. When something happens that I see as context, I spend more time using the BASH process to move forward. [You will learn all about the BASH process in chapter 4.] Most of the time, doing this doesn't take any more time, but when it does, it is totally worth it.* ◀◀◀

> *When I face a difficult situation, I try to remember that*
> *this too shall pass, and I try to make the best of it.*
> – ELIZABETH HILDEBRAND DOBBS

As a STEAM-powered girl, the ability to know the difference between content and context can be applied to every aspect of your life. Many of the women we interviewed said that they realized how important it is to know the difference, and it gives them power over each situation: when to stand up strong and when to lighten up, leave a positive mark, and move on. You are more powerful when you recognize a situation for what it is and choose how you want to deal with it.

Writer and editor Debra Englander says, "Look for solutions. I was a reporter at *Money Magazine*, and I had arranged for people to sit on a panel. Several people cancelled at the last minute, but when I complained, a writer I worked with dismissed my complaints and said, 'If you're going to succeed at the magazine, then you need to present solutions, not problems.' I've kept that advice in mind throughout my career."

STEAM Principles in Careers

A lot of the women we interviewed explained how they use STEAM principles in their everyday working lives. You may be amazed at the diversity of uses these important principles encompass. Here are some of the stories they told us.

Ramonita Martinez is a registered nurse whose career encompasses all aspects of STEAM. "Science is one of the most important aspects of my work, since I need to have knowledge of biology, microbiology, anatomy, and chemistry to understand how the human body functions and the reasons why we get sick. Technology is important because I use a lot of equipment to treat and heal illnesses. As we make advances in the medical field, knowledge of technology becomes pivotal in a nursing position. Engineering plays a big role, too, because of the machinery involved, such as MRI machines, medical scopes, and lifesaving monitoring equipment, and there are some procedures that can now be done using the assistance of robots. Knowledge of how the equipment operates will help one be a better nurse.

"Being a nurse is a special art, so we need to have more than an educational degree; we must also have a passion and enjoy helping people. Most of the time we deal with patients and their families in very painful or difficult situations. People tend to be most vulnerable when they are sick and afraid, which everyone responds to in a different way. Nurses need to understand this, to not take anything personally, and to be creative in helping patients deal with their illness or symptoms in the best way possible. Math is also important to nursing, especially when we give medications to patients. We must calculate dosages accurately in order to properly take care of our patients; a simple miscalculation can result in death. We also need math to read and interpret laboratory results and equipment values."

Julia Cherushevich says that art allows her to build an engaging product. "Art helps to make the inventions we develop engaging and accessible to other people."

Another example of how necessary the arts are to design is printed circuit boards (PCBs), which are the electronic boards that are in all of our electronic devices. When PCBs were first invented and manufactured, their components were mounted and soldered by hand, which was very delicate work. The best people for the job were elderly women, who sat making PCBs in the factories at large tech companies! These companies found that the sewing, knitting, and crocheting these women had always done had given them the dexterity, attention to detail, and methodical nature that was optimal for making PCBs. In fact, in Miami, Florida, in the 1960s, many women worked in the textiles factories, but when those factories went overseas, these women went to work on PCBs. Their experience as seamstresses as well as sewing and knitting for enjoyment made them the best-suited candidates for the job.

Test engineer Alexandra Sanz-Guerrero says that working with difficult people can also be an art, and longtime nurse Ave Brouckaert points out, "We are all influenced by visual art and music, and they both can help patients with recovery and healing."

Patricia Fors notes, "Math is an essential skill in my field of human resources. I use math to interpret affirmative action/equal employment opportunity reports, create turnover reports, determine salary bands and benchmarks, and speak intelligently with businesspeople who are very number focused. I also use math to perform measurements and statistical analysis to determine the viability of HR practices and programs, and much more."

Julia Cherushevich is a software engineer and cofounder of PriveHealth, a company that seeks to educate healthcare employees about good cybersecurity etiquette. She says that every single part of STEAM is essential for her to be successful. "For all of our company's goals to come together for our clients, we combine behavioral psychology (science) and pedagogical principles with a web-based platform (technology, engineering) to create an engaging product (art) in order to drive measurable behavioral change (math) in our users."

Rachel Winsten is an engineer for a major theme park in Florida. She is constantly working to identify potential safety problems. During this dynamic process, she must utilize all aspects of STEAM. "I use science when I conduct industrial hygiene surveys. I apply technology and engineering when I inspect construction sites and attractions. I use art and math when I look at blueprints and design plans."

Lindsay Bartholomew says, "As an exhibit developer, I may be working in any given area of science, but I also think creatively about how to present those ideas to a general audience. In my mind, the pieces of STEAM are all interconnected. There is creativity inherent in science in terms of how we ask questions and how we design a way to figure out answers, and there is a process and way of thinking involved in any artistic endeavor. I see art in science, and I see science in art."

Pediatrician Bianca Soto says that STEAM "forms the backbone of medicine. Science and math provide the basic principles to understand the pathophysiology of diseases, calculate medical dosages, understand laboratory findings, and so on. Technology is now ingrained in medicine, and facilitates how we practice. The electronic medical record allows us to see information from prior visits. Engineering provides tools and surgical devices that help our patients survive. The art of medicine is also paramount in communicating with families and adapting those principles to individual cases that differ from textbook examples."

Lisa Winter designs and builds enclosed camera systems for tower cranes. She explains, "STEAM is present in everything I do, from picking materials and components to calculating drive speeds and the aesthetic design of whatever I'm building. For me, it's all one big problem that I'm trying to solve. I don't separate it into math, engineering, and art. I like to design with all of it in mind—a balance of form and function."

Xyla Foxlin is the cofounder and executive director of a nonprofit called Beauty and the Bolt, a company centered on the idea that "brilliant is beautiful," and "aims to make learning engineering easy, inexpensive, and accessible for anyone." She is also a creative engineering consultant. She says, "Engineering and art are the same thing, in my mind. They're just creative solutions to human problems, emotions, and life."

Entrepreneur Amanda Davila says, "My path has taken me through every element of STEAM. Starting with medical school, then design, and now entrepreneurship, I was able to harness what I have learned and put it together in a company that I can call my own. For example, in order to start my cosmetics line, I had to collaborate with scientific laboratories and study the science behind ingredients and their benefits in order to create the formulas that are the foundation of my line. I also had to put my artistic and technological talents to work in order to design the logo, branding, and visual identity of my company as well as build an e-commerce website through which I could sell my products. Analyzing data about the website, how users interact with content, and what drives them to purchase is all part of engineering new and innovative ways to have a successful company."

On another note, engineer Angeline Gross remembers this story from middle school: "Ms. Drucker was my no-nonsense, tough-as-nails math teacher who taught me pre-algebra, algebra, and geometry. I remember walking into her homeroom on the first day and seeing her in sunglasses and an all-black outfit with the words "Queen of Mean" (a statistics pun) embroidered on the back. The amount of homework she assigned certainly warranted the title, but I quickly realized why she did this: she wanted to instill the discipline, rigor, and grit we would need someday to take on problems bigger than solving for x. One day, a fellow student asked, 'When will we ever use the quadratic equation in real life?' Without skipping a beat, she replied, 'You're in my classroom, and this *is* real life!'"

STEAM Principles in Everyday Life

Be open-minded. You never know what you'll learn, discover, or who you will meet.
– ANDREA CORNEJO

As you read earlier in this chapter, every aspect of STEAM can be used to come up with solutions. After you start practicing and using these tools and principles, you will begin to use them as an automatic response to the challenges you face. You will slow down, assess what is going on, and then look at the options you have to find a solution. You will be able to figure out the best course of action to take, given the circumstances. You won't necessarily have fewer problems, but compared to other girls your age, you will be able to face them calmly and fearlessly. You will be able to breathe, calmly look at what you are facing, and then manage whatever it is.

This ability becomes stronger and more natural the more you use it and the older you get. Speaking of getting older, the problems and challenges you will face in the future will have greater consequences. Since you will have started applying STEAM tools and principles early on, using them will be second nature, and you will have access to finding solutions for whatever comes your way. For instance, you will need to decide which classes to take next semester, or how to deal with a girl who is bullying you, or even something as simple as which party to go to on a Saturday when you have more than one invitation.

Our interviewees told us time and again that they wished they had these tools when they were teenage girls so they could have better dealt with the turmoil they faced. Ramonita Martinez says, "I have to say that my first years in school were not that happy because of bullying. My family was very poor. I went to school barefoot because I did not have any shoes. There was a boy who would make fun of me and throw his spinning-top toy at my feet, causing them to bleed. I never said anything to my parents because my father was very strict, and I did not want to create any issues or give him a reason to think I was not behaving in school."

The more you, as a STEAM-powered girl, practice and use these tools, the more your confidence will grow. Other girls will recognize that you are breezing through your trials and tribulations, while they will feel like the wind keeps blowing them around and around. This will create opportunities for you to share some of the simple tools that leave you feeling more in control of your own happiness.

You do not have to be in a STEAM field to benefit from STEAM's core skills and mindset. A STEAM mindset will enable you to approach problems from all angles and give you the ability to think critically on your feet.

Attorney Elizabeth Turner studied environmental science and policy as well as earth and ocean sciences during her undergraduate years, then focused on environmental law in law school. She found that her experience in the STEAM fields gave her the necessary skills to get where she is today. She says, "STEAM activities, primarily robotics, helped me learn to approach problems from all angles and to think critically on my feet. Those are crucial skills for a lawyer. I also gained confidence in my abilities."

Studying STEAM subjects allows you to develop specific skills that will serve you all your life, no matter what you choose for a career. Angeline Gross notes, "Even if you decide that a full-time career in a STEAM field is not for you, you will have gained a set of skills that include complex problem solving, creativity, cognitive flexibility, and decision making."

The basic skills and principles of STEAM are applicable in any field and in life in general. As you learn more about being a STEAM-powered girl and applying STEAM-powered principles, you will be able to handle any challenge that comes along, and you will be a role model for other girls, too. You are becoming a leader!

CHAPTER 3
You Can Be a
STEAM-Powered Girl

The STEAM-powered girl mindset is the ability to approach problems from all angles and to critically think on your feet.
– ELIZABETH TURNER

Women have always been at the forefront of making discoveries and inventions, and we will continue to change the world. You have limitless talent, intelligence, and imagination, and it is up to you how you want to use them. The opportunities for women are endless; you just have to power your dreams, and they will power your future.

Lisa Winter notes the importance of girls and women in STEAM: "Seeing a powerful woman at work gave me the strength to do what I wanted in life without second-guessing if I was allowed to do so as a female. If that woman could go after her dreams, why shouldn't I?"

The History of Women in STEAM

You might sometimes hear that there are no female inventors, scientists, or engineers. However, throughout history women have been right next to their male counterparts, doing incredible things. They were STEAM-powered girls long before it was a thing.

There are countless SHE-roes for you to discover and learn from. The women we mention in this book are just the tip of the iceberg. While there is always room for more brilliant women to discover, invent, and create new and exciting things, the reality is that such women have always done so.

Hypatia of Alexandria was a Greek philosopher, mathematician, astronomer, and inventor in ancient Egypt. She was also considered a wonderful teacher; she taught mathematics, philosophy, and music, and had students from all over the world.

Caroline Herschel, born in 1750, was a singer before she became an astronomer. She was the first woman to discover a comet and to have her work published by the Royal Society of London. She also earned a medal from the Royal Astronomical Society.

Marie Curie was a physicist and a chemist. She was a pioneer of the study of radioactivity, the first woman to win a Nobel Prize, and the only person to win the Nobel Prize in two different sciences.

Monica De Zulueta was the first female engineer hired in her department at NASA, and one of the first Hispanic engineers at the agency, working on communication for shuttle and payload processes. When she interned at the National Oceanic and Atmospheric Administration (NOAA), she was the first female engineering intern hired for the Office of Aircraft Operations. Ms. De Zulueta says, "There are so many women throughout history, and around you, who have something to teach you, especially if you are interested in STEAM fields. Use the skills of a scientist to look, research, and discover many of the women who have made incredible contributions to science and the world we live in."

We have compiled a list of many more women scientists and inventors to inspire you in appendix B, "STEAM-Powered Women in History."

WHAT IS A STEAM-POWERED GIRL?

Being a STEAM-powered girl is not just about your abilities; you also have to be persistent.
– MIRANDA AUFIERO SMITH

A STEAM-powered girl has the tools to navigate her world using science, technology, engineering, the arts, and math. She uses these tools in a way that makes her feel in control of her life, stay in the present, and be powerful enough to create a future in which she is in charge of her life, no matter what happens.

A STEAM-powered girl is always learning. No one will ever know everything, because things are always advancing and changing, but a STEAM-powered girl knows how to find the answers to questions and solutions to challenges. She develops the skills she wants and needs in order to solve anything that comes her way. A STEAM-powered girl isn't intimidated by technologies, techniques, discoveries, subjects, or challenges because she knows that there are ways to master anything new that comes along.

A STEAM-powered girl is persistent. When she is taking a tough subject or working on a challenging project, she keeps going and keeps trying. When she is told no, she keeps trying and applying. Sometimes a no is the universe's way of saying not yet, you aren't ready, or this isn't meant for you.

A STEAM-powered girl knows that she will not only survive but thrive by using her talents, the tools she has learned, and her indominable spirit. She will make her world a better place because she knows how to conquer anything.

Technical account manager Lindsey Fischer tells this story: "My mom taught my sister and me basic life skills so that we could be independent in the future. We didn't need to rely on someone else to take care of us because we could do it ourselves. She was a working mother and raised three kids. She didn't baby us. I once went with her for Take Your Daughter to Work Day, and I was so bored while I was there. She told me that I needed to do well in life because I didn't want a boring job like she had. That always stuck with me."

Elizabeth Turner says that a STEAM-powered girl is one who "knows herself, is self-aware, owns up to her mistakes, steps into her achievements, and is proud and honest." That means *you* are a STEAM-powered girl!

DEFINING YOURSELF

"Of course I know who I am. I have been me all my life." This is what a lot people say when asked to define themselves. Do you spend time looking inside to see who you are in relation to others? Do you know what your passions are? Do you know what you like and don't like? What are you good at? What you want to do? What you want to stay away from? If you could look ahead five years from now and be anywhere, doing anything, where would you be, and what would you be doing?

Possibly one of the hardest things you will have to do in your life is to define yourself, but it will set you up for how you live your life. If you think of yourself as smart, then you will radiate intelligence. When you walk into a classroom, your posture will be straighter, and you will look like you command the room. If, on the other hand, you feel like one of the dumbest people in the room, your posture will be slouched, and you will slink to the back of the room, hoping not to be noticed.

Corporate president Caroline Loor says, "My mom told me, 'It doesn't matter what you do—I don't care if you're a garbage collector—but be the best.' That really stuck with me. I pride myself on being the best at anything I do, from waitressing in college to running insurance agencies. My dad also gave me great advice. He said, 'Go to sleep being proud of all your actions that day, and if you're not proud, fix it.' This is a hard one, but it's a great one to live by."

There is a saying that beauty is in the eye of the beholder, and standards of beauty around the world are quite diverse. There are places where skinny women are held as the standard of beauty, and places where skinny is considered unattractive. Why? Because the local social culture thinks that way. There are places where dark eyes and dark skin are considered the highest form of beauty, while a few thousand miles away, women with blond hair and blue eyes are considered the ultimate beauties. The social culture of any area—people—decide what is beautiful.

How do you currently see yourself? No matter what age we are, we hold ourselves up to certain standards: I *should* wear these kinds of clothes; my hair *should* look like this; I *should* have this piece of electronics, I *should* post something on social media. Who created those standards, and why do you believe them?

Think about the most beautiful person your age. Think about the smartest person you know in your age range. Think about the most successful person your age. Now consider yourself. If you were standing next to the most beautiful person, would you feel more or less beautiful? What about the smartest person? The most successful person? Why do you think you would feel that way? Are you actually more or less beautiful, successful, or intelligent than any of these people? How do you determine whether you are more or less? Let's take a look at why you might feel certain ways about yourself.

How you think about yourself is based on judgments you make about yourself. We're going to let you in on a little secret. The most successful people, no matter what their success is, *define* themselves as successful. The smartest people in the world define themselves as smart. When people define themselves as something, they *are* that something.

Jessica Vineyard is a great example of this phenomenon. Jessica is a chemist by education, an astronomer by hobby, and an entrepreneur in practice. She says, "In my early fifties, I owned a successful spa, but when the economic crash of 2008 hit, I lost my business and had to start over from scratch. I thought about what my passions were. I had always loved books and reading, so I decided to become a freelance book editor. I had no idea how to go about starting this new career, but once I made the commitment to go for it, I immediately starting telling people that I was now a book editor. My friends and acquaintances asked me how I was starting a new career in a field I had never worked in before. I said, 'I don't know yet; I'm just doing it!'" Jessica first defined herself as a successful editor and *then* figured out how to make it a reality. She now has a successful career doing something she loves. Recently she traveled all over the world for four and a half years, since she can work on her laptop from anywhere!

Think about a time when you felt beautiful. Maybe you were having a great hair day, your skin was glowing, and your outfit totally rocked. You walked out your front door, and you knew you looked awesome. Your definition of yourself was "beautiful," and the energy you were projecting was beauty. You felt good, and that feeling carried you through your day in a different way than if you had walked out your door feeling ugly. Defining yourself as beautiful, even if you aren't conscious of it, impacts your day in a positive way.

Now think of a time when you thought you just looked OK. You walked out your front door and met up with two friends. When they saw you, their eyebrows went up, and they let you know that you looked fantastic. Think about what happened: your opinion of how you looked that day was *meh*, but your friends thought you looked great.

There can be a big difference between how we see ourselves and how others see us. We tend to see only our flaws or focus on a particular flaw, like a bump that might turn into a pimple, but other people see the bigger picture. Two things are at play here. First, how you define yourself lays the groundwork for how you carry yourself through your day. Second, everything is an "inside job." In other words, no matter what you see or hear about yourself on the outside, you can always choose how you feel. You can know that you are uniquely beautiful and have skills and talents that nobody else has. You can carry yourself tall, filled with the knowledge that you are magnificent; all of that comes from inside you. You can choose to believe or not believe negative and positive things you hear about yourself; you can choose to be happy and filled with joy and peace, no matter what is happening on the outside.

In a moment you will do an evaluation that will give you insight and perspective about yourself, showing you how you truly see and feel about yourself. Sisters Sara and Jennifer have fun doing the exercise once or twice a year. They know that they change a lot throughout a year, and they are aware of positive changes in each other.

Nola here. Before I start this exercise, I always dress in a way that is flattering to me, because I am going to look at myself in a full-length mirror for part of the evaluation. I feel better when I am wearing my "good" shorts or an outfit that I really like. This exercise can be done throughout your life to keep a handle on how you see yourself and where you are in your life experience. After you finish, sharing the results with someone who knows you, loves you, and has your best interest at heart, like your best friend, can be a fun and helpful thing to do. In fact, I have done this with my sisters and my best friend. Doing so is helpful because those who love us see even more of the good things about us and can help us fine-tune the results, as we can for them.

◀◀◀▶▶▶

The evaluation focuses on looks, intelligence, social skills, and more, so it is important that you are as open and honest with yourself as possible. The snapshot of who you are in this moment will help you evaluate what you want to do and be, and more importantly, to appreciate who you are right now.

Set aside plenty of time so you don't have to rush. Let's get started.

EXERCISE: PERSONAL EVALUATION

First, take three slow, deep breaths to bring yourself to a place of calmness and focus. Next, read each step, and think carefully about your response. Write your responses in your journal or notebook.

* Stand in front of a full-length mirror. Carefully look at your whole head, then your hair, your forehead, your eyes, nose, cheeks, mouth, chin, and neck. Describe in detail what you look like as if you were telling someone who cannot see you. Explain the colors, textures, shapes, sizes, and other physical characteristics of your head in as much detail as you can.

* Look into your eyes. Look beyond their color and shape. What do you see behind your physical eyes? What are the expressions looking back at you? Are your eyes kind eyes? Are they critical eyes? Are they the eyes of your best friend? Describe the nature of the eyes you see looking back at you.

* Step back from the mirror and look at your body as a whole from the neck down. Write down a description of your overall body. Is there a difference between what you

see when you slouch and what you see when you stand up straight? Do you give off a different vibe depending on your posture? Write down what you observe.

✳   This step can be a little more difficult, so please be as honest as you can with yourself. Make a list of the parts of your body that you aren't thrilled with at the moment. (At your age, you have the advantage of knowing that your body will be changing for the next few years.) For each item on the list, write down two things that are *positive* about that body part. For instance, if you write down "breasts" because you do not like their size, two positive things you could write down are that they are in the middle of changing and that they will someday feed your child.

Nola here. When Lizzy and I were doing this exercise, she told me that she has been self-conscious about her upper arms for her whole life, so "upper arms" went on her list of body parts she doesn't like. For the two positive things about her upper arms, she wrote that her arms are strong, dependable, and always serve her well when carrying things; and that her arms were strong enough to carry her on crutches when she needed them.

✳   This step is more fun. Write down three body parts that you think are your best features. Then write down at least two positive things about them. (Seeing all the wonderful aspects of your favorite features will help you see more than two positive aspects to your not-so-favorite features. Write them down, too.)

Now that you have evaluated your physical body, it's time to move on to your intelligence. Take three deep breaths as before, then write down your responses to the following questions.

❋   Do you think you have a lot of common sense?

❋   Do you think you have street smarts?

❋   Are you classroom smart? In other words, do you have an easy time in school? Which subjects are easier for you? Harder?

All throughout your life you will have strengths and weaknesses. Do not get discouraged if you believe that you are not as smart as others. You have many talents and skills that make you unique. Often the people who are at the top of the class now do not go on to be successful in later life; it all depends on their ability to navigate through life's challenges. The fact that you are reading this book and doing this exercise gives you a huge advantage in being successful at whatever you choose.

One of the ways that young people navigate through life is by expressing themselves through both speech and social media. It is important to be aware of which method you are most comfortable with when communicating with others.

❋   When you communicate through speech, do you feel more comfortable speaking face-to-face or over the phone (calling, texting, video chatting)? Does it make a difference who you are speaking to? Make a list of the people who you feel most comfortable speaking with face-to-face. Why is talking in person with these people easy? Are you more comfortable with them because you don't think they are judging you?

❋   When you feel comfortable speaking to others in person, are you aware of your feelings of confidence? When you are uncomfortable speaking to someone one-on-one or in front of a group (like in class), does your heart beat faster? Do you get nervous? Do you feel like you are not good enough?

Who decides if you are good enough? Write down your observations and answers to these questions.

Now think about your social media use, and answer the following questions. Be honest. This is only for you.

* Do you post frequently on social media?
* What kinds of posts do you make?
* Why do you post what you post? Is it to impress others? To keep up with your friends or other people you want to impress?
* How do you feel after you post something?
* What do you enjoy or not enjoy about posting on social media?

Your answers to these questions should give you insight into how you see yourself. Review your answers every six months or so to see how your perception of yourself, and you as a person, change over time. Then do the evaluation all over again.

Nola here. An important part of a joy-filled, successful life is to be comfortable with who you are, right here and now. One of the most important things I have learned in my life is that no one is everyone's cup of tea. In other words, there has never been a human being that appeals to everyone.

◀◀◀▶▶

No matter what you change about yourself to please others, you will never please everyone. That being said, always be true to yourself. Hundreds of years ago William Shakespeare wrote, "To thine own self be true," and it is as true today as it was back then. Assess yourself from time to time to see if you are the person you want to be, then walk tall and know that you are a unique and marvelous young woman.

FOLLOWING YOUR PASSION

Don't do things because you think you are supposed to or are expected to; do what you love.
– JACKIE GARCIA DE QUEVEDO

Life is full of extraordinary possibilities. Since the beginning of time people have had thousands of ideas to be passionate about. It is from people following their passions that we have the wonderful inventions and lifestyles of today. If no one had thought that having indoor bathrooms would be cool, we all might still be going to an outhouse in the middle of the night. If a whole lot of people hadn't been passionate about women's right to vote, we would not be able to voice our ideas and vote for representation that we support.

Leonardo da Vinci had many, many passions. He followed and acted on them so much that many of his ideas and inventions are still a part of our lives four hundred years later. He is a great example of the idea that while it is important to be passionate and to follow those passions, you do not have to get stuck on one particular passion for the rest of your life.

Nola here. This brings up a concept that is near and dear to me, called "Living the Dash." When a person from the past is quoted or referenced, two dates are typically included: the date of their birth and the date of their death, separated by a dash. For instance, you might see "Leonardo da Vinci, 1452–1519." Have you ever thought about the dash between those two important dates? It represents all of who the person was, their entire life journey. Leonardo da Vinci's dash represents an abundance of life experiences as a result of his many passions. What will your dash look like?

My sister, Yvonne Anderson, always loved biology. She was accepted to medical school and dental school, yet she eventually became a nurse who treated patients with severe eye diseases. People thought she was crazy not to go to medical school, but she was happier as a nurse, attending to people in the way she did. She says, "Never let anyone tell you what you should be passionate about or what you should study. You are always better at something when you are passionate about it."

◄◄◄►►►

People who are passionate have an effect on others because passion is contagious. Think about a time when you came across a person who was bubbling over with excitement about something; you couldn't help but be infected by their energy.

Rachel Winsten says, "Spend time pursuing your passions, whether they be art, travel, music, sports, or something else. Life is short, and tomorrow is never guaranteed. I believe it is very important to have a balanced and well-rounded life. I have resigned from jobs because they were too demanding or required too much time away from friends and family. A work-life balance is so important. I found that without this balance, you can burn out and become resentful of your employer and job. Find activities and people that you enjoy outside of work. Even if you are pursuing a true passion in your job and love going to work every day, try to make it home for dinner."

Lizzy here. I was quite overwhelmed when I was applying to colleges because there were so many different schools and programs to choose from. My mom gave me the advice to focus on what I wanted out of life. College is a means to an end; it is a stepping-stone on the road toward what you want to achieve.

I wanted to go to a school where I could get a scholarship and not have to take out student loans. I knew that I wanted a small college where I could make a lot of close friends, and not feel like I was lost among a large crowd. I also wanted an engineering school that had a strong entrepreneurship program and offered classes in Shakespeare. When choosing a college, I focused on the type of experience I wanted and what my priorities were. That led me to my eventual decision and what became one of the most fulfilling experiences of my life.

◄◄◄►►►

You can use all your skills together in what you do. Jessica Vineyard says, "I worked as a chemist after college and taught astronomy as a hobby. These skills now serve me well in my current career as a freelance book editor. It is surprising how often I use my knowledge of astronomy. For example, if someone describes a full moon in a starry sky in their story, I point out that a full moon actually washes out most of the stars from view, and you can't see all those stars! A science background is highly useful for editing many, many kinds of books."

Amanda Davila says, "I am an entrepreneur with several startups in different industries. I went to medical school to become a dentist in my native Costa Rica, graduated with a minor in dental surgery, and practiced at an American-owned dental clinic before moving to Los Angeles at age twenty-four to pursue my passion: fashion and design. While I was in the United States, I earned my degree in fashion design and merchandising. I did an internship as a visual merchandiser, setting up the visuals and artwork for store windows, and I also designed the clothing and accessories displays in the store. After a while I found I was passionate about skincare, which led me to start my own skincare line, Good Skin Club."

Amanda followed her passion and loves running her own company. Follow your passion, and you will never regret it.

TRUSTING YOURSELF

There is no right path, only the path that is right for you.
– LISA WINTER

Trusting yourself is an important life skill, and you will develop it over time. Ave Brouckaert says, "Don't let anyone tell you that you can't do something. Faith will get you through the toughest situations."

You must have faith in yourself. It is an important aspect of being a STEAM-powered girl. You must have faith in yourself when you are trying to prove a hypothesis or discover something new. You must have faith in yourself when you are inventing something that has never existed before, or when you are trying to break a glass ceiling and accomplish something no one (or no one who looks like you) has done before. All of these things take a strong belief in your abilities and the confidence that you can do anything. If no one has done something you really want to do, then it is your destiny to be there first.

Caroline Loor tells this story: "I was quite the tomboy, and started my first 'company' buying and selling basketball, baseball, and hockey trading cards; I was one of the guys, so to speak. Unfortunately, all of the boys I had a crush on would tell me how they liked one of my friends.

"I couldn't get on the boys' basketball team, so my sister and I started a girls' team in seventh grade. I had styes (painful red bumps at the base of an eyelash) for the majority of my time in middle school. I was made fun of for being a tomboy and for my styes. Ultimately, this teasing built my character and helped me gain a sense of humor because I learned to make fun of myself before someone else did."

The bad things that happen to you will make you more resilient and help to build your character. If you can trust yourself and learn to laugh at yourself and the craziness of life, then this resilience will help you get through many challenges in life. As a STEAM-powered girl, the more you use the tools you are learning, the stronger you will become, and the stronger you become, the more you will trust yourself.

Ana Victoria Soto-Quintela says, "I have been bullied and disrespected, and one notable experience was during college. I was studying biomedical engineering (BME) at the number-one ranked college for this major at the time. There were many times that I struggled to make good grades. I was no longer the top of my class, and I had to work very hard to pass. During those first couple of years, many of my fellow classmates told me I should quit, since the odds of my graduating with a degree in BME was unlikely considering I was a female, and a minority to boot. This just made me study harder, but it was a difficult time in my life."

We all have an instinct inside that is there to serve us. It is the feeling you feel, or the inside voice you hear, that lets you know the right thing to do. The more you trust yourself to know the best solution for the problem at hand, the louder and stronger that feeling or voice becomes.

You are an intelligent, powerful young woman, and you have the ability to make good choices. Trust yourself!

THE IMPOSTER SYNDROME

Befriend your imposter syndrome.
– XYLA FOXLIN

The imposter syndrome is when you doubt the worth of your accomplishments, or when you feel like you are a fraud or liar. It is when you think that everyone is going to figure out that you aren't as smart, cool, hardworking, or good as they thought.

The imposter syndrome is really common; almost everyone feels this way at some time or another. Most people with imposter syndrome don't talk about it because they want to keep it a secret. They believe that they are the only ones who know how incompetent or not-smart they actually are, and they still feel this way even when they have tons of accomplishments that show otherwise.

Nola here. I felt this way a lot when I was younger, especially when I wasn't sure I could reach any of my goals. One thing that helped was learning that I wasn't the only one who was scared or felt like they had tricked people into thinking they were smart. Learning the term "imposter syndrome" was a big *aha!* moment for me. When I realized that it was just a feeling, I knew I could use my STEAM tools to analyze it, learn from it, and then decide how I wanted to react to it.

◀◀◀▶▶

Lizzy here. I have also felt like an imposter. I have learned some ways to remind myself to believe in myself and my accomplishments, and that I, like everyone else, am constantly learning and growing.

It was my first semester of freshman year in college. I had just started my Physics 1 class and was working really hard. I was enjoying the class and wanted to do well. The class consisted of a lecture with a hundred students, a conference session with just twenty students, and a lab. I went to all of my classes, did all of my homework, talked to the professor when I had questions, and did a practice exam, which I got an A on. By the time the first test came around, I thought I was ready. I knew that I had to prepare because I had always been a poor test taker. I was always slow and had a tough time finishing. In middle school and high school I worked hard on my homework and projects so that they would make up for any bad test scores. This was how I got good grades.

Now, just like I had always done, I prepared and studied hard for the exam. I was confident I was going to do great. I was working through the problems and thought I was doing well. Then the teacher called out "Time!" The test was over, but I was only halfway done! How was that possible? I knew the problems, had prepared, and had worked hard. I was devastated.

When the test results came back, I got a 50 percent. I left the class crying. Later, I talked to my professor to understand what I did wrong on the test and what I could do to improve. He was confused, too. He saw that I had answered the questions I had finished correctly. He had also seen my homework and practice exam and knew that I had studied hard.

My professor worked with me to prepare for the next test, and I took the practice exam once again. I reviewed all the test-taking techniques I had learned in middle school and high school, which were designed to help students take tests faster. Then came test day. I got going as fast as possible, working through all the problems I could. This time I wore a watch and followed the time carefully.

As I worked through the test, I noticed that I had only ten minutes left, and I was barely halfway done. I rushed through the rest of the test, hoping that I had enough to at least get partial credit here and there. Then I heard "Time!" and the test was over. I felt defeated but hoped that I did better than the last time. I got a 60 percent.

This was when the imposter syndrome hit me hard. I had worked hard and done everything I needed to do, and I still wasn't smart enough to finish a test that I had studied and practiced for. Many other students had taken only half the time and got A's on their exams. I felt like I was in way over my head; clearly, I wasn't smart enough for this school. I had even received a scholarship, but they were obviously wrong about me, because I was already failing my first class, and it wasn't even October.

My mom had taught me to finish what I started. There were a few weeks left in the class, and one more test to go. Again, I talked to my professor, and again, he didn't understand why I couldn't finish my test. He then asked, "Do you have any accommodations?" I had no idea what that meant. He explained that some students need extra time or resources to be able to effectively complete their work, especially exams. I told him I had never had accommodations, but I did have a learning disability when I was younger, and because of it I am generally a poor test taker. He suggested I go to the disabilities office.

I learned that I would need to be specifically tested to confirm whether I needed accommodations or not, but that particular testing could wait until school break. The woman at the disabilities office approved extended time on tests until the end of the term to see if it helped me perform better. I was confused and assumed it wouldn't help much, but I was desperate to try anything. Deep down I felt that it might not help and that it would only prove what I already knew: that I was an imposter. I wasn't smart enough and wasn't cut out to be an engineer.

As the last physics test approached, I had done my homework, worked hard on the practice exam, and studied the night before the test. The students with extended time took their tests in a room separate from the rest of the students. I wasn't the only student who needed extended time, which made me feel a little better. I got my test and began working through the problems. I worriedly watched the clock, but I could see that I had plenty of time. When I was halfway through the test, I panicked and looked at my watch. Still plenty of time. I finished the test, looked at the time, and had a few minutes to spare. I couldn't believe it!

But I was still worried. I was not going to relax and be happy until I knew whether I had passed the test, which would mean the difference between passing the class and having to retake it. A few days later, I got my test back and got an A. I did so well on the last exam that between that test and my homework grades, I got a C and passed the class. Now, I know that a C is not always a grade to celebrate, but that physics class was one of the most important learning experiences of my life. I learned that perseverance is extremely important. I learned to not be embarrassed to ask for help, and that I am smart enough. I left the imposter syndrome behind when I learned that I really can do what I set out to do.

> *Look for alternative approaches in as many directions*
> *as you need to until you find the one that works.*
> – AMY CUTTING

You are smart and capable, but it's OK if you have moments of self-doubt. We all question our abilities sometimes, but the important thing is to remind yourself of all the wonderful things you have done, all the talents you have, and all the times when you overcame an obstacle. This will help you in those moments when you feel like you can't do it.

Xyla Foxlin points out, "Grades. Don't. Define. You. I got B's and C's in high school and college, I didn't go to an Ivy league college (which also means I'm not slammed with debt), and I am doing just fine. In fact, I think I had more opportunities because I spent time developing my portfolio and skills and doing things I am passionate about instead of just cramming for exams. If school isn't your thing, don't let that stop you. Just build cool things!" Focus on your passions and skills and developing your portfolio. (Portfolios apply to artists and engineers alike.)

Architect Carolina de la Horra remembers, "I was told by other students that the first of nine exams I had to take for my architectural boards was going to be the easiest. They said that everyone passed this first test and that it would prepare me for the following eight 'hard' exams. When I received notice that I had failed the first test, I was taken aback. I felt like a fraud, an imposter. If I couldn't pass this test, there was no hope for passing the others.

"I refused to study for the next, 'harder' test, which I had already registered and paid for. A couple of weeks before the test, I figured I would open my books since I was already invested. When exam day came, I took the test quickly, without any pressure, since I was sure to fail, so I was shocked when I passed. From then on, I realized that putting too much pressure on myself would block my subconscious from doing its job. I passed all nine exams within the year. You know more than you think you do, and you must trust your gut."

Let the impostor syndrome push you to be a better version of yourself, but don't ever let it tear you down.
– XYLA FOXLIN

Overcoming Doubt

Nola here. When robotics was starting to become popular in schools, I was one of the leaders in creating a curriculum and getting robotics teams started across the United States. I was invited to speak at a convention in San Jose, California, and many major robotics executives and other folks were coming to talk about advancements in technology and to see where the future of robotics was going.

I was invited because I was known for my passion in sharing engineering and robotics with students and teachers, and I had worked with the owners of BattleBots—a television series featuring fighting robots—to create one of the first hands-on curricula for in-school and after-school robotics. The people attending the convention would need employees to work for them in the future, and the students who were building robots were the people they would be hiring.

I grew up with seven siblings, so I learned early on that I have to speak up in order to be heard. When I worked for BattleBots, I traveled all across the country asking manufacturing associations to support robotics education in their communities. I spoke to hundreds of people at schools around the country. I was never nervous about speaking. I was always confident in what I was saying and sharing.

I arrived at the convention prepared and ready to go. On the morning of my session, I started to panic for the first time. I went into a stall in the ladies' room and stood there wondering if I was going to get sick to my stomach. What was going on? Suddenly, all of the work I had done to prepare for this session didn't seem like enough. I thought, *Who do I think I am? There will be people from Toyota and Honda headquarters from Japan. I am supposed to speak to important executives from GM, Chrysler, Ford, and other major manufacturers. I'm just a mom from Miami!*

I started talking to myself to calm down, and then, as I always do in situations that are out of the ordinary, I started to pray. I asked God to send me some angels to help me out. Suddenly, I got calm and started asking myself questions as if I were a mirror image of myself. *OK, Nola, what is the worst thing that could happen out there today?* I had a whole list of things that could happen: I could split my pants, I could fall down on stage, the audience could laugh at me and say things like, "You don't know what you're talking about," or "Go back to Miami," or "What a waste of time coming here to listen to you." They could throw tomatoes at me. I even thought they could escort me off the stage and out of the convention center.

After I had exhausted all of the horrible possibilities, I asked myself if I could live through any of them. Reluctantly, I realized that even though it would not be pretty, I could make it out alive if any of those scenarios happened. I would be humiliated, embarrassed, horrified, and upset, but yes, I could live through it. Then the most important question popped into my head: on a scale of one to ten, how likely was it that any of these things would actually happen? I had to admit that it wasn't likely that one of the bigwigs from Honda or Ford would have tomatoes in their pockets ready to throw at me. It wasn't likely that anybody would yell nasty things at me or that I would split my pants; I had bought a new outfit for the trip, and it fit really well.

Next, I listed all of the preparation I had done for the presentation. I had done my research, put together an awesome PowerPoint presentation, and rehearsed my script over and over again. I asked myself how prepared I was on a scale of one to ten, and whether I would be able to present the information professionally. I had to admit to at least an eight, if not a nine. I felt so much better. I realized that I had created all this fear in my head for nothing. I left the ladies' room a lot more confident and happier than when I had gone in ten minutes earlier.

The audience loved the presentation and was excited to hear about the kids and the robots. I had been allotted five minutes for questions, but the audience asked question after question for more than fifteen minutes. All of my fear and upset were for nothing. Not one of the terrible possibilities happened, and in fact, on that scale of one to ten, my presentation was a 10+.

Now, whenever I start to doubt myself, I ask, what is the worst that could happen? Could I live through that? How prepared am I? More often than not, I am prepared and things move forward smoothly.

◀◀◀▶▶▶

EXERCISE: OVERCOMING DOUBT

Nola's exercise is a proven way to get through even the toughest of times when you are experiencing self-doubt or fear. First and foremost is to understand that all of what you are experiencing is in your head. Remembering this gives you the power to deal with anything that comes your way.

Follow these steps to calm your mind and overcome doubt in the moment.

* ❋   Take three deep, cleansing breaths, and then choose to be in total control of the situation.
* ❋   Clearly define what you are afraid of or in doubt about. For example, you doubt that you will pass the test, or you fear you will give a poor presentation.
* ❋   Assess your situation. Did you study for the test? Do you know the material? Are you prepared for and have practiced the presentation?
* ❋   On a scale of one to ten, how likely is it that you will actually fail the test or mess up the presentation?
* ❋   List all of the things that could go wrong. "If I mess up this presentation, the audience will throw tomatoes at me, or someone in the audience will yell out that my information is wrong." Go through all of the possibilities, and ask yourself if you would be able to live with even the worst, craziest outcomes. (Maybe you would be embarrassed for a few weeks, but you could live with it).
* ❋   Go through the list again, and on a scale of one to ten, honestly decide how likely it is that any one of them would happen. If you paid attention in class and studied for the test, the likelihood of failing is incredibly small. If you prepared and practiced your presentation, the likelihood of doing well is high. Even if you do fail the test or give a bad presentation, your life will go on. Imagine your life five or ten years from now, and think about whether failing the test or giving a bad presentation will be a big deal.
* ❋   Give yourself a pep talk. Talk to yourself as if you were talking to your best friend. Take three more deep breaths,

and remember that you are in charge of what you think, what you believe, and how you allow your thoughts to affect you.

This technique works with every situation you can imagine. Nola has even used it on little kids who are afraid of walking down a dark hallway in their house!

CHANGING DIRECTION

Many of the women we interviewed changed direction at some point in their life, career, or profession. Follow your instincts. Who you are at twenty or thirty or forty or fifty is going to change. You will have many experiences that add to your talents and to yourself as a powerful woman. Follow your passions, use your instincts, and apply the tools you have as a STEAM-powered girl (and later as a STEAM-powered woman), and make the choices that honor you and what you know are best for you.

Angeline Gross didn't know what she wanted to do when she was in school. She says, "The best way to describe my middle school experience is 'trying.' I was trying to understand how my body was changing. I was trying to figure out who my real friends were. Above all, I was trying to figure out who I was and who I wanted to be. It seemed like so many of my peers had found their niche. They played volleyball or practiced a musical instrument, or they participated in scouting or student government. Even though I enjoyed school and got good grades, people made fun of me for not having a life. It seemed like everyone had already figured out what they wanted to do and were actively pursuing it, while I was left in the dust.

"In hindsight, I can see that this was irrational and overdramatic. Child prodigies are a rarity, and teenagers often end up dropping their activities and interests (even ones they've done for years) and trying new ones. But in my myopic adolescence, I didn't see that. Instead, I saw the walls of my friends adorned with trophies, ribbons, and plaques that recognized all that they had accomplished in their brief youth. I felt the walls closing in, and if I didn't get good at something now, I feared I would never be successful. So, I tried everything: soccer, dance, guitar, scrapbooking.

"In retrospect, it was a good experiment; I quickly sorted what I liked and what I didn't. Eventually, I found my way to Nola and Bill's warehouse-turned-workshop in Miami, Florida, where I discovered that I could channel my talents in math and science into engineering and build some really cool robots along the way. (Lots of girls and young people got their start in STEAM-related professions at Nola and Bill's workshop!)

But even if that hadn't happened and I had taken longer to figure out my calling, I wish I would have known that that would have been OK, too. It's OK to not know what you want to do, and it's OK to change your mind a thousand times even if you do know. Changing your mind doesn't mean that you will never be successful, it just means that you're taking the time to get to know yourself. Eventually, you'll find your way. As philosopher Zen Shin once wrote, 'A flower does not think of competing with the flower next to it. It just blooms.'"

Everyone does things in their own time. Don't worry about competing with other people; you don't know what their journey looks like. You will figure it out and get to where you are meant to go.

Interior designer Andrea Cornejo says, "I have a bachelor's degree in political science from the University of Florida. At thirty years old I decided to go back to school and study interior design at the Art Institute in Fort Lauderdale. I was working full time and incurred a lot of debt going back to school, but sometimes you don't follow your passion when you are young because you haven't discovered it yet.

Looking back, my passion for interior design started at a young age, during all the years I played with my Barbies, creating environments for them to live in. I didn't have a Barbie house, so I used things I found around our house. As I got older and cleaned people's houses to earn spending money in high school, I would sometimes rearrange their furniture."

Take pride and do your best in everything you do; no job is too small or unimportant. Every job, every person, and every experience can teach you something, so it is important to try your hardest. Focus on making yourself proud, and if you aren't proud of what you're doing, change course or fix it until you are. Don't be afraid to change course, because most people don't know their true passion when they are young.

Your Talent Stack

Success is about getting every tool possible into your tool belt and choosing whatever path you like.
– ELIZABETH DE ZULUETA

Scott Adams, the creator of the *Dilbert* comic, coined the term "talent stack" to describe a group of skills you have cultivated that, when put together, make you unique and one-of-a-kind. As Adams explains, "When you add in my ordinary business skills, my strong work ethic, my risk tolerance, and my reasonably good sense of humor, I'm fairly unique. And in this case that uniqueness has commercial value."

A talent stack is not about being the best or perfect at any one skill. The magic is in picking the skills and talents that speak to you. When you choose and design a group of skills just for you, you become extraordinary. You may not be perfect at any one thing, but when you become good at several different things, you become exceptional.

Scientist Amy Cutting says, "I never set out to find my career; it happened over time. I worked for the Naval Undersea Warfare Center in Newport, Rhode Island, after graduate school because it was one of the few places hiring at the time. That work led to projects supporting defensive system development. I succeeded there in a couple of roles, and while I missed working in the field of blue water oceanography, I learned that I loved testing and evaluating many different varieties. When I took a new role with the Coast Guard, I hoped my subject matter would change back toward environmental science. In the end, my defense background proved more unique and useful to the organization, and I have continued in that vein. I was disappointed at first, but getting great results from hard work is incredibly motivating. I see how my particular skill set has allowed me to succeed where others have failed. I have become passionate about my work, even though the field is not my passion."

A stack is made of combining several things together to make a bigger, more complete group, like a stack of books. By reading the stack of books on your shelf, you combine the knowledge and lessons from one book with the knowledge and lessons of the others. This helps you gain multiple perspectives and new, interesting ideas because the things you learn from all the books and information you read will interact and build on each other.

A similar concept in the technology field is called the "technology stack," or tech stack for short. A tech stack is a group of programming languages and software tools used in the development of a website, app, or digital product. The more tools and languages one knows, and the more one can build one's personal tech stack, the better products one can build.

As you learn new things and grow your tech stack, you will improve yourself and increase your ability to solve any problem. Continuously growing your tech stack and learning technology tools helps you work toward the goal of being "tool agnostic," which means that you have many tools and skills to choose from and are not dependent on only a few. By continually growing your stack, you can choose the best tool or skill to address a particular problem.

> *I am cautious about applying technology. I always look for ways to ease the work of the users instead of applying technology for its own sake.*
> – MONICA DE ZULUETA

This is how a talent stack works: you first focus on the skills that you already have and that make you unique; next, if there is a skill you admire and want, you add it to your stack, especially because it is important to keep growing; and lastly, by combining your many unique skills and creating a unique skillset, you become extraordinary.

Sara and Jennifer were curious about what talent stacks they could possibly have, being so young.

▶▶▶ *Jennifer: The more we know ourselves, the more powerful we are, so Sara and I were excited when we did an exercise to find out what our individual talent stacks were. Both of us are individuals and have different talent stacks. Remembering this helps when we want to do something new, or even when someone tries to make us feel bad about ourselves.*

I was working on a group project in my class, and Heather, a girl in my group, said that I didn't know how to write an answer for the project. I had completed my talent stack exercise, and I knew that one of my strong points is that I am a good public speaker because I can come up with answers to questions and communicate effectively. So I was confident that I could write the answer for our group project.

I thought about what Heather had said, and I realized that she was trying to micromanage the group because she was insecure and nervous about her own grade. I felt stronger and knew I could do it. I also felt sorry for Heather, who wasn't aware of her own talents and skills. If she had been, she would know that she didn't need to feel insecure, and that by using good communication and working as a group using all our individual talents, we could all get good grades. But because she wasn't feeling good about herself, she tried to make me feel bad about myself and my abilities. ◀◀◀

▶▶▶ Sara: I had a similar experience. I spoke up in a group project to let people know that I have lots of different skills and talents that I am proud of, and that I am spending time developing them to be even stronger. ◀◀◀

▶▶▶ *Jennifer: Both Sara and I understand that we are given talents and that it is up to us to appreciate and use them, yet we don't want to brag or be stuck up. But we also know that it would be a slap in the face to our creator to ignore or deny our talents. We realize that if something isn't in our particular talent stack, then we can add it if we want to.* ◀◀◀

Knowledge is power. Being aware of something allows you to use that information in different ways. If your talent stack includes an ability to speak in public, for instance, then you might volunteer to be part of a project that helps homeless people by raising awareness of what is happening in your town. You might give a presentation at school or a commission meeting that brings awareness to others and helps the project come to a successful conclusion. If your talent stack includes the ability to create social media materials, then you can be part of the same project in your own way with similar results. Being of service empowers people and encourages them to do even more. Both Sara and Jennifer have experienced how good it feels to volunteer and help others in various ways.

Every time you make use of your talents, you strengthen them. If you become aware of a talent you have that is not particularly strong or a talent that you lack, you can find ways to strengthen it or add it to your stack. You are in charge; you can add to and create the stack that you desire.

EXERCISE: FIND YOUR TALENT STACK

This is the exercise that Sara and Jennifer completed. It is fun and will add to your strength as a STEAM-powered girl.

You will need a quiet place, a willingness to be honest with yourself, and your notebook or journal and a pen.

Sit down and slowly take three breaths, in and out. Let go of any negative ideas about yourself that others have told you or that you believe, that might keep you from tapping into the truth of who you are.

In your notebook or journal, write down all of the abilities and talents that you think are good, important, or worthwhile; for instance, being a confident person, being able to speak in public without getting flustered, having a talent for mathematics or science, having a love of nature or animals, being able to cook, and being able to read a map. Include personal qualities, too, such as being dependable, trustworthy, and honest; being able to look at a problem and immediately see possible solutions; and being able to bring order to a messy room or desk. Making this list can take a while, but just keep adding to it.

On a clean page, write a list of the qualities and talents from your first list that you already possess. Be totally honest.

On the second list, put one checkmark in front of the qualities and talents that are light in strength, two checkmarks that are medium in strength, and three checkmarks in front of your strongest talents.

Start a new page in your journal or notebook. Next to the items with one checkmark, jot down a short description of each quality or talent. Go on to the items with two checkmarks and then the list with three checkmarks. Look over the three categories of checkmarks and see if you are satisfied with your self-assessment. Is there anything missing? Does the list reflect the person you think you are?

Now, it's time to share this list with someone you trust, because people who love us usually see even more good things about us than we see in ourselves. Have this trusted person make notes about your qualities and talents.

You can also swap lists with a friend who has done the first steps already (but don't work on those steps together). Look over the list that your friend made, and see if they have something on their list that you did not see in yourself.

▸▸▸   *Jennifer: When Sara and I completed this exercise, we saw that there were some pretty cool things that we both had, and some things that one of us had and the other did not. At first I felt a little disappointed that Sara had some talents and qualities that I wanted, but then I realized that Sara could be part of my team and help me develop the talent stack that I wanted, and I could help her, too.* ◂◂◂

Next, write a description of yourself from a second-person point of view. For instance, looking at herself as if she were someone else, Jennifer started her description like this: "Jennifer is a quiet, sweet young girl who can be counted on to do what she says she will do, when she says she will do it. She has many positive qualities and abilities, like her ability to use technology to create technical papers for science projects and social media."

Write as much as you need to in order to describe all the qualities and talents that you listed earlier. After you're done, read your second-person description of yourself. Does it describe the true you, the you that has so many possibilities to succeed in whatever she desires? Are you impressed? Later you might decide that you don't want to spend more time on one or two of the items. If so, just put them on the back burner for now. You are in control of your life, remember that!

Lizzy here. One of my teachers told us a story that has stuck with me since fifth grade. It was about a girl who had to deal with a lot of problems, but she knew that even if she couldn't control what was happening on the outside, she could absolutely control her reactions to them and what went on inside of herself.

◄◄◄▶▶▶

Now go back to the first list you made, of all the positive qualities and talents you could think of. Are there any that you like but do not have? This is your opportunity to expand your talent stack into areas you want to explore.

▶▶▶ Sara: I really like robotics, but I am not knowledgeable about engineering. I would like to be on our school's robotics team, so I have decided that I will read and learn about robots by next year. Knowing that one of my talents is the ability to learn quickly makes me pretty certain that I can learn enough by next year to join the robotics team. ◄◄◄

Since we are all in charge of our own lives, where we want to go, and what we want to be, it's handy to keep your talent stack journal up to date. You can add to it by writing down what you think you want to do or be in life, and note where you have complementary talents that can make accomplishing that easier.

Creating your own talent stack gives you power in many ways. You recognize that you have innate talents that you were born with, certain qualities that are yours and yours alone. That in itself is powerful. Take it one step further, and you can choose what talents, skills, and qualities you desire and then develop them with the help of others.

TEN THOUSAND SANDWICHES

Nola here. My experience as a STEAM-powered woman is based on the idea that she sees a need and fills it. A STEAM-powered woman pulls her community together when she sees that her talents can be used to support others and empower them to be the best version of themselves.

When my youngest son was in kindergarten, I was visiting a local bookstore while I was waiting to pick him, his brother, and a neighbor boy up from school. On one of the walls was a collage of black-and-white photos of homeless men, women, and families digging through dumpsters for food. I asked the woman at the register if they were pictures from New York or some other faraway place. "No," she said, "they are from right here in Miami. Those people live less than five miles from here." I was horrified! I had no idea. I was sure that no one else I knew had any idea, either.

When I got to the school, I spoke with Mrs. Nunez, my younger son's teacher, about how unbelievable this was. She asked me if I would speak to her kindergarten class about this. I agreed and went back to the bookstore to get more information about the homeless situation in Miami.

There was so much I didn't know. Even though we have homeless shelters in Miami, there are countless people who, for whatever reason, do not make use of the facilities and all they offer. The woman told me that her church took it upon themselves to start ministry, where they made peanut butter and jelly sandwiches for the homeless. They also filled clean milk bottles with drinking water, then drove around and distributed them to people on the streets. I learned that some of the northern states would purchase bus tickets for the homeless in their cities and send them down to Miami in the winter so they wouldn't freeze. Our population of homeless would expand in the wintertime.

I told Mrs. Nunez what I had learned and that I had borrowed a book from the bookstore about the homeless and their challenges. She and I came up with the idea of having her class make some peanut butter and jelly sandwiches to deliver to the church for their ministry. It sounded like a great, simple, noble idea: twenty-five kindergarten kids making seventy-five peanut butter and jelly sandwiches . . .

I thought it would be a good idea to make the sandwiches right before the children's lunchtime so they could get a little feeling of what it was like to be hungry. When we were almost finished, one of the girls shouted at the top of her lungs, "Albert is *eating* the sandwiches he just made!" Albert was a hefty little boy, and there he sat at his table, the remnants of a peanut butter and jelly sandwich all over his face. I asked him gently, "Albert, what are you doing?" He said, "I am *so* hungry!" I asked the rest of the class who was hungry, and all of them raised their hands, secretly hoping they would get a sandwich, too. I used the opportunity to explain that these sandwiches were a gift to the people who might not have eaten for two days or more. One of the students asked if we could pray for all of the people in the world who were hungry. Their prayer was the most precious thing I had ever heard. They went to lunch with a new appreciation for the food they ate.

Word got around the school, and soon every single teacher had asked me to speak with their students about homelessness and hunger. All of the students wanted to make peanut butter and jelly sandwiches and fill water jugs with clean water for the ministry. A friend and neighbor who taught at an inner city school told me that her kids felt like they were not included in our good works. To remedy that, our local food store donated bread, peanut butter, jelly, and sandwich bags for the kids at her school to participate. One of the local television stations got wind of the project and came to the school to film the kids singing the Phil Collins song, "Another Day in Paradise." The kids were so excited when they saw themselves on national television making sandwiches for the homeless!

That Thanksgiving, one of the second-grade students stopped her family dinner and asked the twenty people at the table to close their eyes and think about how it would be if they had no home, no food, and no blankets. She told them about the homelessness problem and then asked everyone to go home after dinner and get as many blankets and sweaters as they could to start a drive for the families who would soon be cold. When a child brings information to the awareness of adults, it speaks volumes.

A few years ago I ran into two girls who were part of the peanut butter and jelly project. They had been first-graders when they made sandwiches for the homeless. They said that making the sandwiches was a lot of fun at the time, but the residual impact it had made in their consciousness was deeply imbedded. They have since volunteered at the local homeless shelters at different times, and have looked with love on the people on the streets who appear to be homeless. They are true STEAM-powered girls!

◀◀◀▶▶▶

A STEAM-powered girl takes the initiative to act on what moves her. She gathers resources she needs to get the job done, and empowers others as she goes about her life. Using your STEAM-powered tools, you can double or triple your power to make a difference in your own life and the lives of others.

We will close this chapter with seven items that career educator Cathi Cox-Boniol believes are important to be a STEAM-powered girl:

1. Invest in relationships. The relationships you make in your life will enrich your potential in ways you can't even imagine. Make your relationships count; cultivate friendships, establish partnerships, collaborate freely, and invest richly in others. Love beyond yourself, and learn to love others so you can love what you do.

2. Take advantage of opportunities. Be committed to learning, but also seek out opportunities for service, support, and encouragement. Developing a strong heart for service will often take you further than your academic prowess.

3. Yearn for more. Don't settle for the bare minimum. Develop a work ethic that supports a thirst for digging deeper, stretching further, and reaching higher. Desire excellence; it is what everything should be built upon.

4. Allow yourself to grow academically, socially, politically, and spiritually. Put each of your talents to good use. Take advantage of each guide you have along your path, and challenge them to help you grow.

5. Build your future. Building upon the foundation you already have requires thought, planning, hard work, revision, repair, replacement, and more. Decide what you want your life to look like, then make sure you are adding tools to your toolkit that you will need to manage the design your future requires.

6. Ask questions and then search for answers. You are going to be required to make informed decisions, and the only way to do that successfully is to be fully informed.

7. Find your voice and validate who you are. Use the tools you gain to certify, for yourself and for the world, who you are. You are going to have to count on that person for the rest of your life.

Becoming a STEAM-powered girl takes focus and practice, and it is absolutely worth it. It will positively impact you for your whole life. It starts with defining yourself, knowing who you are, trusting yourself, and knowing that you have unique gifts and talents that no one else has. You have the tools to solve any challenges you face, and you have a team of people to support your passions, your projects, and your life.

CHAPTER 4
How to BASH Your Challenges

It's not impossible, it just hasn't happened yet.
– LINDSAY BARTHOLOMEW

Henry Ford famously said, "Whether you believe you can do a thing or not, you are right." In other words, how we see the world is how the world will be for us. Some of the happiest people are those who face the most difficult challenges, and sometimes the people who we think have it all are not happy. The answer lies inside; happiness is a choice.

You are now ready to learn how to use the tools of the STEAM-powered girl. In this chapter, you will learn how to solve a problem using BASH, a process we developed that is based on a process that NASA and successful leaders in business use to find solutions to both simple and complicated challenges. You will be able to use the BASH process for any kind of problem you will face at any time in your life. You will also learn the importance of a team, the group of people who strengthen and support you in your adventures and experiences.

As you navigate your way through life, you will always have some kind of challenge or problem to deal with, from the smallest, such as where to go on vacation, to the greatest, such as making decisions that will affect thousands of people. Through it all, you will have access to the simple, yet profound, steps to take to resolve anything you face.

We are excited for you to learn and practice with these tools. You will start to look at the world in a whole new way: the STEAM-powered girl way.

The Importance of a Team

Shared joy is a double joy; shared sorrow is half a sorrow.
– SWEDISH PROVERB

You now have a good idea of what your talent stack is and what your strengths are as a STEAM-powered girl. Being aware and honest about who you are and what your innate talents and skills are is important in moving forward, but you also want to start building a team to support what you want to do.

Middle school was hard for Dottie Fauerbach, as she was very shy and quiet. She felt alone and didn't confide in her friends or peers. She didn't have a team, which made everything harder. On the other hand, Lisa Roberts had a solid team around her. She says, "I had a teacher in eighth grade who complimented my work in front of the class. She used my science folder as an example of how everyone should be doing theirs. Since she made me feel so good in front of the other students, I excelled in her class and got a recognition in science at the end of the school year. Her praise was a small token of positivity, but I never forgot her gesture." Lisa's teacher was on her team.

Look around at the world today, and you will see that almost everything of value is accomplished not by one but by many people. Most big solutions to challenges are discovered and developed by teams of people who have different talent stacks. For example, for an electronic device to be invaluable to users, all of its processes must work flawlessly. It takes many people to make such a device and bring it to users, including designers, electrical engineers, computer engineers, and the marketing team. Each person on the team has different qualities and strengths that make their input important to the success of the project.

When a project manager starts putting a team together to produce a final product, she thinks about what she wants the final product to look like. She makes a list of the various team members she will need to cover all facets of the project at hand. For example, if the end product is a gadget that keeps track of social events, the team would consist of people with different skills than team members for a project to create a blood testing kit to detect viruses. Each project requires a team of individuals with specific skills that contribute to the success of the end product.

Any successful person will tell you that it would have been impossible to get where they are without a team of trusted individuals who have their best interests at heart. Jennifer has a good example of pulling together a team to help her apply for and get her dream internship.

▶▶▶ *Jennifer: I wanted to apply for a summer internship in a doctor's office, and I wanted to turn in the best application I could. I knew I needed to put together a team of people to help me get the internship, and I thought a lot about who could help me.*

One friend's mom works in a doctor's office as a receptionist, and another friend's mom is a doctor. I let them both know that I had an opportunity to be considered for an internship and that I wanted to be prepared for the interview. I asked them separately if we could meet to go over the application, and they both invited me to their homes. I wanted to make the best use of my time, so I created a list of questions to bring and brought the application with me. I think one of the most important questions I asked was what it would take for me to stand out among the other applicants. It was exciting, because I now had both of them on my team.

Next, I went to my school counselor and asked her to give me pointers about filling out the application as professionally as possible. I then asked my parents what they see in me that would make me a good candidate for the internship. As a STEAM-powered girl, I discovered that each of these people has a unique relationship with me and unique perspectives on the internship application. They all had different ideas of how I could be a great intern, which I was able to use later during my interview.

By the time I turned in my application, I felt well prepared and knew that I had a team of people who were behind me to support my dream. Oh, and yes, I got the internship. ◀◀◀

Consider a situation or challenge you are dealing with, and think about the talents or qualities you want from people who could be on your team. In your notebook or journal, make a list of the positive qualities you have to help you with the situation or challenge, then make a list of the qualities that you know would help in finding a solution to your challenge. Who do you know who has what you are looking for?

The most important thing is that you don't get stuck in your doubt. When you do have doubt, it is helpful to review and reflect on all of the positive aspects of who you are. Look at the doubts, write them down in your journal, then list all the reasons they are not valid.

GATHERING YOUR TEAM

Luck is what happens when preparation meets opportunity.
– SENECA, ROMAN PHILOSOPHER

Having a general team is a really good idea. Your team can be a casual group of people you know who are helpful to have on hand when life happens. Everyone has unexpected things come up, and it really helps to have someone to turn to. Think about who you already have on your team, people you feel comfortable talking to about private stuff, such as good friends, an aunt, a teacher, or a counselor. It is good to have these names written down for times when you have a whopper of a challenge. You can look at your list and know you are not alone.

We heard many stories from the women we interviewed about the importance of personal teams. For example, when Bianca Soto really needs to talk to someone, she turns to her mom. She says, "There were times in the past when I was disrespected and felt sad and lonely. I would confide in my mother, who always gave me good advice. She told me to keep my composure and not retaliate. I would also feel better by turning to my true friends, who respected me."

Lindsey Fischer found that having trusted friends around her helped her through school and beyond. "I felt bullied regularly, mainly about my weight, but I was also the tallest kid in middle school until eighth grade, when the guys started to catch up. I probably didn't deal with it in the healthiest way, but I just tried to avoid conflict by keeping to myself and focusing on my schoolwork. I had a very close friendship with another girl in my grade, and we regularly hung out and stuck together. 'Awkward' was my middle name until my mid-twenties. I was fortunate to find folks who were just as awkward as me, and we formed great, long-lasting friendships. In fact, we were in each other's weddings."

When you are going through tough times, it helps to focus on what you are good at, what you love, and the people who love and support you, even if there are only a few of them.

Xyla Foxlin shares about her personal team. "I'm really lucky to have the most bad-ass mom and aunt. My mom is an immigrant who put herself through graduate school in architecture here in the United States. She barely took a maternity leave when she had me, and she worked insanely hard. She is now a fashion-forward interior designer, and taught me that I could fight like a girl and look like a lady. My aunt had an Ivy League science degree, but she realized that academia wasn't for her. She moved to Vermont and started a fencing school and a folk band. She never wore dresses, and she taught me to 'keep up with the boys.'"

There are many different types of women in this world. Some will look like you, dress like you, and have all the same interests as you, while others will be your complete opposite. However, regardless of path, style, or background, they all can serve as examples in your life, teaching you lessons that are unique to but no less important than any of the others. They can also be the perfect people to have on your team.

Amy Cutting depended on her family as her team during a hard transition. "When I took my current job, I returned to work full time after nine months of working part time. I hadn't had to travel for work for six years in my prior position, but my new job required occasional travel. The transition to this new schedule was not smooth for my family. I felt like I was failing my husband and kids because I didn't have the time to devote to them that I had before. I felt selfish, and to be honest, taking the new job was a selfish decision. It has taken time, a lot of hard discussions, and sacrifices from my husband and family to make my job possible. I'm grateful that we worked through it, and I am so much happier to have a job I love and find meaning in. It makes me a better person, even though it sometimes causes day-to-day stress."

Like Amy, Alexandra Sanz-Guerrero's team is really important to her in her personal life. She says, "One of the best things I've ever done for myself is to surround myself with people who care about me and support me on good days and bad. I firmly believe that people aren't meant to do things on their own. It is our friends, family, and community that help us work through the excitements and pitfalls of day-to-day life. Once you find the people who will stand by you, hold on to them, and don't be afraid to open up to them."

Lizzy here. You can see the common theme in all of these stories about having a team: seek out people who make you grow. My great-great-grandma used to say, "Pick friends who always give to you," by which she meant people who give you joy, motivation, kindness, confidence, good examples, and good influences.

◀◀◆▶▶

Now we want to introduce you to a foundation that will help you in all situations: the BASH process. This process is a tremendous tool that you can use to face your challenges head-on as a STEAM-powered girl.

THE BASH PROCESS

Progression, not perfection.
– ELIZABETH DE ZULUETA

We have created a four-step process, based on a system that two NASA engineers shared with us, that works for every type of problem, from having a bad hair day to choosing which electives to take next year.

The BASH process can help you decide which schools to apply to, whether you should work this summer and get paid or take an unpaid internship, and know what to do when the wrong guy asks you to the Christmas dance.

▶▶▶ Sara: Once I get over the initial *uh oh!* on a bad hair day, I automatically go into the BASH mode: 1) I take a few deep breaths to calm down; 2) I assess the situation (bad hair); 3) I find a solution (put it up in a clip and mess around with it until it cooperates); then 4) I make it happen (a little hair spray usually tames it). Sometimes I add an extra step: 5) I smile when it's done! ◀◀◀

The BASH process is four simple steps: 1) *breathe*; 2) *assess* the situation; 3) find a *solution*; and 4) make it *happen*. That's it. Four simple steps that you can learn right now. Let's look at each step in depth.

1) **Breathe.** Deep breathing is one of the most powerful ways to bring the body, mind, and spirit together to face what you are dealing with. When you consciously focus on your breath, you stop thinking about whatever is challenging you at the moment. When you take deep breaths, you oxygenate your body. The oxygen will feed your brain so that it can process information and help you to find a solution.

Start your breath by inhaling through your nose to the count of four. Hold the breath to a count of seven, then exhale through your mouth to the count of eight. Do nothing to the count of three, then start the process again. Doing this short process at least three times consciously and slowly will help you access the innate power you have to find solutions to your challenges, big or small.

Try it now. Take a slow, deep breath; inhale for four; hold for seven; exhale for eight. Repeat twice more.

2) **Assess** the situation. Now you can assess the situation at hand and unemotionally evaluate it. Assessing a situation narrows down the challenge to something that is more manageable. Sit down with a pen and your journal, and write down everything you can think of about the challenge at hand. Look over your answers and summarize them into one or two sentences.

Step back and look at the situation from a different perspective. Be as logical and impartial as you possibly can. If there is another person or group involved in your situation, assess what each party contributed to the situation. Look at the situation from all sides, as though you were a judge sitting in a courtroom. A judge doesn't always say who is right and who is wrong. In many cases, she tries to find a solution in which both sides can agree, even if they aren't completely happy.

If you're still having a problem assessing the situation, you might try a technique that many successful professionals use when faced with big challenges. In the evening, when you are ready to go to sleep, say this statement out loud: "I want to have a restful sleep tonight. While I am sleeping, I know that a win-win solution will come to me by the morning. When I wake up, it will be at the forefront of my mind."

Nola here. I keep a pen and paper beside my bed so I can write down any ideas that come to me in the middle of the night or when I wake up. Sometimes I just record a message in the Notes app on my phone. (There have been so many times when I tried to read what I wrote in the middle of the night, and I think, *whaaaattt? What did I write?*)

◄◄◄►►

3) Find a **solution**. Once you have narrowed the assessment down to a simple statement, you are more likely to find a solution. Often, a solution will pop up immediately. If not, start writing down possible solutions, no matter how crazy they sound. This exercise can spark the

creativity that will bring the perfect solution into focus. If a solution does not become immediately apparent to you and you have the time, share the assessment with someone whom you trust, or else you can sleep on it. Most problems have many solutions, and you get to pick the one that resonates with you the strongest.

Making a list of possible solutions empowers you to see that there are many ways of solving a problem. Let's say someone is bullying you. You have assessed the situation and realized that she bullies you right after lunch, when you are on your way to class. You write down some possible solutions: you can take another route to class; you can talk to a teacher and explain the situation so he or she can speak to the bully; or you can ask the teacher to have both of you sit down together to discuss what is going on. Any one of these solutions can lead to putting a stop to the bullying. Always try to find a solution that is a win-win for all people involved.

4) Make it **happen.** Once you have determined the best solution that you are comfortable with, take action on it. Sometimes the action is as easy as speaking to the other person face-to-face, explaining what you believe happened, and sharing your thoughts. If the solution is more complicated, write down the steps you need to take in order to make it so.

Sometimes the first solution does not solve the problem. Don't feel like you failed! You simply found one way that didn't work. Look over some of the other solutions you wrote down, and choose another one that you can make happen.

As a STEAM-powered girl, you can use the BASH process to actively make your life better every day instead of sitting around feeling like a victim. You might even be a role model for someone else going through a tough situation when they see you being proactive and making your life STEAM-powered. Every time you solve a problem using the BASH process, you are putting money in your internal bank of self-confidence.

Ave Monaghan tells her remarkable story: "I joined the air force three weeks out of high school in 1971. I eventually trained to be a main frame computer operator, a field that had very few women in it. I didn't work or interact daily with another female until I was almost thirty. I was always good in math, so once I figured out coding and what bits, bytes, and digits were, things clicked, and I became a nerd, pocket protector and all. In the late 1970s I had to learn how the bits and digits traveled across the world using satellites, phone systems, radio transmission, antennas, and eventually even Morse code.

"Around 1980 I was trained as a law enforcement officer, and for three months a year for the next four years I worked full time as a cop. I was the only female law enforcement officer on the air force installation for the first two years. It was nothing for me to work a shift on the computer and then turn around and have to report to the 'cop shop' for another couple of hours.

"When I retired from the air force at age thirty-eight, I had an associate degree in data processing, and I was seventeen semester hours short for a bachelor of arts in resource management. I was finally getting that college education. In 1994 I took a position with the navy as a network system administrator. I had formally moved from centralized computing to decentralized computing, or networking.

"My greatest accomplishment occurred on September 11, 2001. My director's office suite was destroyed by the airplane that hit the Pentagon. My recovery team, all three of us, established a totally operational alternate site by five o'clock that afternoon, and the director was established in another site communicating with the rest of the navy with only one day's loss of data. All of my experience up to then helped me to realize how important it was to have good recovery procedures. The three of us used engineering, math, logistics, and seat-of-the-pants common sense to do the emergency job."

As you can see, using STEAM-powered principles can help you find a way to master any problem or challenge that comes your way, big or small. We always have the potential to make forward progress on all that happens in our lives. There will always be problems, issues, and mistakes. What is important is what you do about the problems: find solutions.

Now let's see how to apply your new STEAM-powered skills to some of the common problems we mentioned in chapter 1.

DEALING WITH OVERWHELM

One of the first steps in understanding anything is knowing what it is and what it is not. From there you can change your expectations of what is challenging you.

The first step to dealing with overwhelm is to recognize it for what it is: it is a feeling that feels like it is going to take over your whole life. In reality, you can get through the feelings and find a way to move forward in a way that helps you become stronger and feel much better.

When you are feeling overwhelmed, remind yourself that you have everything inside of you to take control of the situation and get it handled. It won't always be easy, but the more you are calm and know that you can find a solution, the more manageable the feeling becomes. Remember, you are the master of your life; you are in charge, and you always have an infinite supply of energy and courage to deal with whatever is happening.

Do not boil the ocean. In other words, don't try to do everything all at once. Always keep learning, but choose one segment that interests you, master it, and then move on to another one.
– MONICA DE ZULUETA

Write down in your journal what you feel is overwhelming you. Then apply each step of the BASH process to find a solution: breathe, assess the situation, find a solution, and make it happen. If there are a lot of things that are making you feel overwhelmed, start with the thing that feels the biggest.

Let's see how Jennifer applied the BASH process to help her feeling of being overwhelmed. Her parents, who love her and want the best for her, put pressure on her to succeed in school, but it created a situation that made her feel overwhelmed.

▶▶▶ *Jennifer: I am not very good at art, but my parents pressured me to succeed in that subject. I used the BASH process to deal with the pressure, and as a result, we all are happier at my house. Here is what I did:*

*1) I took a big **breath**—actually, a lot of them.*
*2) I **assessed** the situation: My parents pressure me to succeed in art even though I'm not very good at it.*
*3) I found a **solution**: I can change my attitude about my ability, and maybe I will find that I'm good at some kind of art, such as pottery, drawing, or sculpture.*
*4) I made it **happen**: I started the semester in art class with a new attitude. I decided I would find something in the class that I liked and that I'm good at. Guess what? I discovered that I love sculpture! Seeing the statue inside the block and then making it come to life was so exciting. I'm happier, and my parents are happier, too. They*

are looking forward to owning a sculpture of their own. ◀◀◀
Sara felt totally overwhelmed because she has too many things to do and not enough time to do them. She put the BASH process to work to help her find balance.

▶▶▶ Sara: I really like practicing this process. Here's what I did:

1) First I took a big **breath** to slow down my mind and my thoughts.

2) Then I took a few minutes to **assess** the problem: *I just have too many things to do and don't even know where to start.*

3) After I thought a lot about it, I found a **solution**. I made a list of everything I have to do and when each thing is due. Then I looked at each item to see if there was anything I had taken on that I could let go of without a problem, and I took those things off the list. Next, I rearranged the items and their due dates in order of importance. I also thought about how much time and energy each item would take, and I added that to the list.

4) Here is the payoff: I made it **happen.** I found something simple on the list that I could do immediately, I did it, and then I crossed it from the list. Jennifer taught me that crossing things off a list gives me a feeling of accomplishment and control. Make sure to do two or three simple tasks to get yourself started, but don't get stuck on doing only the simple tasks. ◀◀◀

One thing to be aware of in Sara's last step is that doing only the simple tasks can become a form of procrastination. Use these small tasks to get your day started and to give yourself a feeling of accomplishment, but don't stop there.

After doing two or three small tasks, tackle the hardest, most important tasks next. These are the ones that you wish were already done, the ones at the top of your list. Look at the simpler tasks that you have already accomplished, and ask yourself if you are choosing to skip an important task. If you are, well, we all have those moments. You may not be sure how to accomplish it or even if you can, or you might be intimidated because it is so important. In these moments, starting the task is even more important. You *can* accomplish it. With these kinds of tasks, sometimes you just have to start them for the ideas to start flowing. But once you do, you will be done in no time.

If you continue to struggle, ask for help. Talk to your team. If you can, negotiate more time to complete some of the tasks on your list. Explain to the appropriate person that you have a lot of things on your plate, that you want to be responsible and successfully complete the task, and that you would like more time. Many times, if it is a school project, teachers will work with you to evaluate the timeline and figure out a way to complete it with integrity. (To be honest, sometimes they won't give you more time, but one way to look at this is, if you don't ask, you don't get. You have nothing to lose by asking for what you want.)

When you feel overwhelmed, step back, figure out what is going on, name it, and use the BASH process to empower yourself. Just like any muscle, the more you use the BASH process, the stronger it will get.

Everyone gets overwhelmed, at all stages of life. No matter how successful you are, no matter how old you are, life can be challenging, but you can learn to manage overwhelm. If you work on it now and master the steps to keep it under control, you will be prepared for managing it all through school, college, and for the rest of your life.

EXERCISE: DEALING WITH OVERWHELM

The more you practice any kind of exercise, the stronger you get. Dealing with overwhelm is no different. This exercise is a powerful way to learn to recognize when you are getting pulled into the current of feeling overwhelmed.

Take three breaths with your eyes closed. Think of a time when you felt completely overwhelmed. Write it down in your journal. Feel it like it is happening right now. Does the overwhelming feeling you had then feel like you are feeling right now? Remember that you got through it then; you came through intact. You will be able to get through this situation, as well. Now think about what is actually happening now. Look at it from as many angles as you can. Write down what you think the problem is, clearly describing the situation. It should be so detailed that you could give it to someone who knows nothing about the situation and they would understand it.

Now imagine that the current situation is happening to someone else. Doing this lets you take the emotion out of it and look at it analytically. See how many solutions you can find. There are usually multiple solutions to any problem, so come up with at least three. Take a deep breath, then consider each solution and see which one feels the best and makes the most sense. Visualize that solution happening, and see the problem being solved. Feel what it feels like to have the problem solved. You already know what that feels like. Close your eyes and take three more deep breaths.

Open your eyes. Remind yourself that this exact same simple process is used by smart, successful people to solve highly complex problems. You always have the ability to use the BASH process to find your own solutions. When you do, you will always be in control of what your next steps are to make your life better.

Michele Loor says, "Everyone around you is going to have their own opinion about what you should do and how you should do it. The bottom line, though, is that you need to be able to form your own opinion and decide what is ultimately the best route for you."

Dealing with Bullies

A bully is a person who is a coward on the inside.
– NOLA GARCIA DE QUEVEDO

"She is so cute and adorable!" Seven-year-old Lulu has this effect on many people—until she opens her mouth. Lulu is a chihuahua who is obnoxious and a meanie. She yaps as loud as she can at other dogs for no apparent reason other than to intimidate them. Most of them run away as she chases them down, sometimes chomping at their paws.

Marley is a mixed-breed dog. She is about the same age as Lulu and doesn't bother anyone. She wags her tail when she sees other dogs. Lulu has chased after Marley and yelled at her, trying more than a few times to bite Marley's tail and paws. Instead of being intimidated, Marley just laughs and tries to play with Lulu. Marley is a smart dog. She realizes that Lulu is insecure about herself. She is smaller than most other dogs and thinks that they make fun of her (which they don't). Marley figures that if she doesn't let Lulu intimidate her, Lulu might stop bullying the other dogs.

Marley has the courage and wisdom to ignore Lulu's yaps. She tries to play with Lulu, showing her that she is not going to allow Lulu to get to her. Lulu eventually stopped trying to bully Marley, and little by little, she started yapping less and looked at Marley with admiration. She watched how Marley made her way through life, being kind and choosing to be happy no matter what else was going on.

Have you ever known kids who are like Lulu? They are so insecure about themselves that they feel they have to attack others to make themselves feel better, prettier, smarter, or more competent. Of course, if you asked these kids if they feel insecure, they would most likely deny it, but research has shown that bullies often attack others to try to keep from feeling bad about themselves. Bullying is not usually about the people they bully but about the bullies themselves.

Do you know someone like Marley, who chooses to be happy no matter what? Someone who knows when to go to an adult when they are being bullied in a way that they can't walk away from? People of any age can be bullied, physically, mentally, or emotionally. Everyone has the right to feel safe all the time; nobody has the right to take that away from you.

Amanda Davila remembers, "There were many times when I was bullied during school. The girls were specially mean to me, calling me names and criticizing me behind my back. The way I dealt with it was by looking for support in friendly places. I would talk to my mom about it, and she would tell me not to let those mean comments get to me because they're not true. I would read funny stories about girls doing magnificent things, and that would inspire me. I hung out with my small group of nice friends, and had fun watching movies with them. We all got bullied at one point or another, but we found out that we were stronger together and that there is always somebody on your side.

"One time I faced the girls that bullied me and told them to stop. I said that they shouldn't be gossiping or saying mean things, that they should be nice. I believe it helped; at least, it quieted them down. More importantly, it made me feel powerful and able to defend myself. After doing that, I realized that I was stronger than their comments and that I could get through it."

A bully is a coward on the inside. Bullies treat others badly because it makes them feel more powerful than the person they are bullying. They pick on people who they think are physically or emotionally weak. They will often puff themselves up by verbally or physically hurting someone who intimidates them.

Sometimes bullies try to excuse their behavior by saying, "I'm only telling you the truth," or "I'm telling you this for your own good," or

"Everyone says the same thing about you," or "I'm just being brutally honest."Being honest is important, but no one should ever treat you with brutality. You may think that the person is telling you the truth, but always consider the source. Who is the person telling you this? Is it a trusted friend, or the girl who is always mean to you in class? If it is someone who is mean to you or puts you down, then that person is not telling you the truth to try to help you; they are trying to make you feel bad about yourself. Such a person may tell you the truth, but they exaggerate it or change it to make it seem worse. They might say it in an ugly way or in the worst light possible, or change its interpretation to hurt you.

For example, let's say you are super excited about the bottle rocket you built for fun over the weekend. You learned about pressure and propulsion, and you worked hard to make your rocket pretty. You were talking about it and showing it to your friends at school, and you felt confident and excited because you love your rocket. A girl who is not nice to you in class came up, called you a nerd, and said, in a mean and sarcastic tone, that the only reason you bring your projects to school is to show off, because you want your friends to know how smart you are.

As she walked away, you began to feel bad and put your rocket away. You were happy and confident and do feel smart, but you also don't want to be a show-off or have your friends think that you feel smarter or better than them. In this situation, the bully said something that is true: you are smart. But she bullied you by trying to turn your ability into something negative and untrue. You are not a show-off, you don't brag, and you don't think you are any better than any of your friends. That mean girl feels bad about herself because she doesn't think that she could make a bottle rocket, so she wanted to make you feel bad. Just remember that a true friend will be excited to see you confident, happy, and will want to see the stuff you work on and are passionate about. If your friends were curious to learn from you, they would ask you to teach them, not put you down. (By the way, if you really do want to make a bottle rocket, check out the instructions in appendix C!)

Forensic scientist Miranda Aufiero Smith says, "The thing that sticks with me the most from middle school is my eighth-grade science teacher, who for some reason would constantly find a way to make me feel down about myself. At one point, she even told me that I didn't have what it takes to become a scientist and that I would never excel in the field. (I would love to have a chance to talk to her now!) I never figured out why she said those things, because I always tried hard to succeed in her class. Though I was young and still had plenty of time to change my career path, I stuck with what I was passionate about."

Miranda shows us that no one else can define you or limit you. You can do anything you want to do! Not even the adults in your life can define what you can or can't do.

I have learned that people will forget what you said, people will forget what you did, but people will never forget how you made them feel.

– MAYA ANGELOU

Let's look at how to use the BASH process to handle a bully: Breathe. Assess the situation. Find a solution. Make it happen.

Standing up to a bully, whether you're eleven or fifty-one, is not easy, but you owe it to yourself to make it stop. When you have assessed the situation and are looking for a solution, you have to remember that you cannot control other people; you can only control how you react to them. You can tell the bully to stop, you can try to laugh it off, or you can ask an adult to step in and stop the bullying. This will help you feel like you are not alone. You can also avoid the places where you are bullied or stay near adults you trust, since most bullying happens when adults are not around.

After you have assessed the situation and decided that the solution is to face the bully by yourself, then take a deep breath, remind yourself how strong you are, and remember that you will be even stronger by confronting this person. Find a good time and place to talk to the bully, then let them know that their words or actions are cruel and hurtful, and that you won't tolerate it anymore.

Remember, you do not have to face your bully alone. You know at least one adult—a parent, aunt, uncle, grandparent, teacher, or counselor—whom you trust and can confide in. Tell at least one of these adults the whole situation, and let them know you need their help. You can also confide in a friend. You might be embarrassed to talk to a friend because you think your friends might judge you or even agree with the bully, but a true friend will want to be there and help you.

Lizzy here. My little brother and I were bullied when I was in middle school, but because I was a girl, they never hit me or broke my stuff like they did to my brother. Because of that, I wasn't sure whether I was being bullied or not. I knew from movies that my brother was being bullied, but I thought those kids were just being mean and making fun of me. I learned that there are a lot of ways to bully someone, including teasing, talking about hurting someone, spreading rumors, excluding kids on purpose, hitting, yelling, and cyberbullying (bullying someone online). Bullying can be both emotional and physical, and it can be tough to deal with if you don't know what to do.

◄◄◄▶▶▶

NEO is a retired certified public accountant. Here she shares her story: "I was bullied when I started at a new school, once by a girl and once by a boy. The girl was kind of tough, and she acted mean toward me, always making fun of me and my heritage. At the time, I didn't understand that she was just afraid of someone new and different joining the class.

"I talked to my mom, and she asked me if I wanted her to talk to the teacher, but I decided to handle it myself. One day I stayed behind after class and approached this bully. I asked her if I had done something to make her mad at me. I think it surprised her that I asked her point-blank, with no animosity, just curiosity. She said no, but she just didn't like me. I said OK, thanks, and how about if we just stay out of each other's way and try to get along even though we are different. From that day on, she didn't bother me anymore, and we got along well when we played softball and other games at school.

"The boy who bullied me sat behind me and would pull my hair. At first, I told him quietly to leave me alone, but he wouldn't, so one day, in the middle of class, I stood up and confronted him. The teacher told me that I had to stay after school for disrupting the class. I said yes, sir, but the boy should also stay for the same reason, because it was his fault. After that, the boy and I became good friends. We still are, and we still laugh when we think back to that day."

Some of the women we interviewed reminded us that we can face bullies as adults, in the workplace or any other place, and dealing with such people is relevant no matter what the age. Patricia Fors says, "You might work with people who think you don't belong, or just don't like you for reasons out of your control. Their attitudes are their problem, not yours. If they try to make it your problem through their words or actions, then speak up."

Rachel Winsten tells this story: "I experienced bullying throughout my grade-school years. Some kids commented on my physical looks, and others made fun of me for being shy. In response, I would just shut down and ignore them. I did not like confrontation, and thought that if I ignored them, they would go away. Eventually, they did go away. Years later, I received an apology from one of my bullies through social media."

How we feel, and how we act based on those feelings,
has a direct influence on how the people around us feel.
– LINDSAY BARTHOLOMEW

Sometimes the best option to protect yourself is to just ignore mean or toxic people. Sometimes simply telling them that bullies don't make the world a better place can make them back off. Whenever you take a positive action, you reinforce the strength of who you are. If you are comfortable, they will feel more comfortable. You influence the people around you by how you respond to them and by showing them how you expect to be treated.

If you or someone you know is being bullied, please visit the website www.stopbullying.gov. It has a lot of information for you, your friends, your parents, and school counselors.

DEALING WITH FAILURE

If you don't make at least one mistake a day, you probably
haven't done anything at all.
– CAROLINA DE LA HORRA

When you make a mistake or experience failure, you are in great company. The most successful inventors, designers, business professionals, sports figures, and anyone else you can think of made quite a few mistakes and experienced more than their share of failures before they reached success in their careers.

The difference between these people and those who don't achieve success is that they did not let their mistakes and failures stop them; they used them to their advantage. Thomas Edison, one of the most famous inventors, found almost ten thousand ways to *not* make a light bulb! Do you think he rejoiced every time it didn't work? We think that he used his own version of the BASH process to move forward and keep trying to find the solution.

Debra Englander says, "I have had to search for months for jobs, sometimes taking steps backward in order to find another position. Although it was hard at the time, these experiences taught me resiliency. Success came later in my career, when I managed a highly profitable business-book program."

Sometimes things happen that will make you feel like you are taking steps backward. That's all right, because failures, or steps back, make you stronger and smarter and more resilient.

Have you ever watched a baby learn to walk? They stand up. Yay! Then they fall down. They get up again and try to take a step, then another, and oops! They fall down. (Good thing they have padding on their bottoms!) They get up again, try to take more steps, and keep falling down, until they finally master walking. Failure doesn't stop them. It didn't stop you, did it? You were a baby once, and you went through all of that. You experienced failure, but you kept going, and now you don't even think about it—you're a pro at walking!

Rachel Winsten says, "I worked in consulting in my first full-time professional job. In one instance, I had failed to properly communicate results to a client. The lapse ended up losing revenue for my company and temporarily damaging our reputation with the client. When I noticed my mistake, I corrected it immediately. In the end, the client thanked me, and eventually we regained their business. This experience taught me the importance of learning from mistakes and that communication is key."

Everyone makes mistakes. The key is to own up to the mistake, communicate the problem, correct it, and learn from it. Failure isn't fun, but it is always valuable if you are smart and use it to move forward. If you let it stop you, then continuing to move in the right direction gets harder and harder. Remember to BASH those feelings of failure so you can move on to success.

DEALING WITH YOUR FEELINGS

Being happy is contagious—not just for others, but for yourself.
– NOLA GARCIA DE QUEVEDO

When you are faced with situations big or small, you can feel like you are flooded with lots of different feelings or with one big wave of the same feeling. We are human beings, and a wonderful part of being human is having feelings. Feelings are important because they can guide us to know what makes us comfortable or uncomfortable in particular situations.

We need to pay attention to our feelings, but we also need to know how much to pay. For instance, if you are asked to talk in front of the class, you might get flooded with panic and filled with fear. You can feel the fear and panic, but don't let them take over. Acknowledge the feelings, and then go through the BASH process. The more you practice this, the sooner you will get good at doing it quickly.

It might go like this: Yes, I'm scared, and yes, I want to crawl under the desk, but I'm not going to let fear run me. I'm going to take a breath, then objectively assess the situation: I need to stand up, go to the front of the class, talk about XYZ, and not look or sound like an idiot. Then I will quickly find a solution: If I act confident and tell the teacher and the class that I'm not sure of what to say, then I won't look like an idiot. If I know what to say or I know the answer, all the better. Next, I will make it happen: I will take another breath, stand up tall, walk to the front of the room, and smile. I will either know what to say or admit that I'm not quite sure. Either way, it will be over soon, and I will have dealt with it like a champ.

Ave Monaghan says, "I attended an extremely overcrowded parochial school in Philadelphia that taught grades one through eight. From first grade on I was good in math, but somehow I slipped through the cracks and didn't learn to read until fourth grade; I could tune out everything around me, to the point where my parents took me for a hearing test. At the beginning of seventh grade I was reading at barely a fifth-grade level, but then I discovered the Free Library Philadelphia, and I immersed myself in books to escape the world around me. By eighth-grade graduation, I was reading at the eleventh-grade level."

If you feel like you have hit a brick wall on a situation, use the BASH process to see if you are being stopped by a real obstacle or by fear. Fear can have strong physical effects on your body. You can feel fear in your stomach or as a tenseness all over your body, or in other ways. Fear can be a powerful force if you let it.

STEAM-powered girls and women acknowledge their fears and do whatever it takes to move beyond them. Others might think that strong STEAM-powered girls and women have no fear, but do not be fooled; everyone on the planet experiences fear. How people handle the fear is what separates the successful ones from those who give in to it.

Nelson Mandela (1918-2013) was an anti-apartheid revolutionary, political leader, philanthropist, and president of South Africa from 1994 to 1999. When he was forty-two, and long before he became president, he was held in a prison in South Africa for twenty-seven years. He chose to not hate his captors, and realized that even in prison he had a daily and moment-by-moment choice to be happy in spite of his imprisonment.

When you feel that life isn't fair and you are feeling down, remember that you made the choice to feel those feelings. This is not to say that you should brush away honest feelings, like how you feel when someone snubs you or makes harsh comments about you; it is normal and healthy to feel hurt. But the powerful way to deal with disappointments is to feel the feelings and then create the way you want to walk through it and past it, like Nelson Mandela did for all those years.

Nola here. At a time in my life when things were very tough for me, a wise person shared with me a statement that has come to help me get through challenges and find solutions instead of allowing myself to feel like I'm drowning in junk. After I told her all my problems, she said, "That's what's so, and what's so is sacred." What she meant was that whatever is happening is what is happening, and it is sacred.

◄◄◄►►►

Don't ever stop trying to reach the next milestone or goal.
– LINDSEY FISCHER

The more you practice the BASH process, the easier it will get. Acknowledge that you have feelings about whatever is happening; know that you can choose different feelings; and then move forward in a way that serves you, builds your confidence, and strengthens your self-esteem. BASH will serve you in every aspect of your life.

DEALING WITH BURNOUT

Burnout is defined as a state of physical, emotional, and mental exhaustion brought on by excessive stress. We burn out when we do not have good methods to cope with the stresses and pressure we feel. Resting and recharging effectively are so important to prevent burnout.

Some of the ways to tell if you have burnout are when you:

❋ feel tired all the time.

❋ are always upset.

❋ are constantly negative about school, work, or responsibilities.

❋ have headaches.

❋ are not able to sleep.

❋ are moody.

❋ easily get sick.

Now that you know some of the signs to look for, the goal is to recognize burnout when you begin to feel it so that you can take the steps to assess the situation and prevent it from getting worse.

We can do anything, but we can't do everything.
– DAN MILLMAN

Lizzy here. Burnout can happen to anyone. I would like to share how I struggled with burnout after I finished high school and how it affected me when I first entered college. I went to a small, all-girls Catholic school that fostered a close-knit environment. We had many clubs and sports, and students were encouraged to try new things and start new clubs, so much so that as a freshman I started and ran the Self-Defense Club. I was the president of a club for all four years, a member of other clubs, a retreat leader, on the robotics and water polo teams, and I helped with many different programs and activities throughout the year. Eventually it all became overwhelming. While it was wonderful to be exposed to so many opportunities and encouraged to pursue them, it was also exhausting. I didn't realize how burned out I was until I started my freshman year of college.

An activities fair was organized during my freshman orientation at Worcester Polytechnic Institute. Every sports team, club, and organization on campus had a table so students could find out about all of the activities the college offered. It was fun, but it was also overwhelming to learn everything there was to do on campus in such a short amount of time. My first thought was, *I don't want to join a single thing. I have been involved in so many clubs, teams, leadership positions, and more that I just want to focus on school and not be packed with activities.*

At first, this was great. I enjoyed not having a packed schedule. I was able to transition to a new state, a new home, a new school, and college life, and make new friends. I went through some challenges that term when I learned that I needed academic accommodations and had to adjust to my classes. I was walking a fine line between being busy and not being busy.

Toward the end of my freshman year, I did join a BattleBots team and was the most successful I had ever been in a robotics competition. For the rest of my time in college, I was careful about the number of clubs or organizations I joined, but I decided not to close off any opportunities. If there was something I thought would be interesting, I would learn about it. If I enjoyed it, I would continue participating, but if I didn't, I would not feel bad leaving, as long as I hadn't made a commitment to anything. If I had committed my time and people depended on me, I would complete my commitment, but then I would evaluate the situation and leave at the end of the commitment. I learned that managing my stress and how much I committed to was as important as how I managed my time. I learned that time is like a room: regardless of how much time we have, we will fill it. The question is, with what?

I still struggle with being honest with myself about how much work I can handle. We are smart and hardworking STEAM-powered girls and women, and we know that we can accomplish anything. But we also need time to read, be with family, rest, sleep, and enjoy music or a hobby just because we love it. I have learned that doing these things really helps because if I don't, I will burn out, which shows up for me as a huge, horrible cold, and I will be in bed for a week with a headache, cough, and sore throat. All I can do is sleep, rest, and drink chicken noodle soup. This is my body telling me that I haven't let myself rest, that I have been working like crazy, and that I sometimes forget to eat at a normal time. It is my body telling me that I am going to rest, and *boom!* I'm sick.

◄◄◄▶▶

When you are tired, your brain isn't as sharp as it normally is, and your body's immune system gets weaker. That is why eating nutritious meals, exercising (anything from walking your dog to going to your favorite dance class to riding your bike with friends), and getting a good night's sleep are excellent ways to mitigate burnout.

If you feel like you are burning out, remember to reach out to your team: speak to your parents, counselors, coaches, and friends. Use your STEAM tools to assess why you are feeling burned out and determine what in your life is most stressful. Then you can assess whether it is time to take some things off your plate so you can cope with your emotions. Having a good outlet for your stress and concerns, such as taking a dance class, doing art, playing an instrument, riding your bike, playing with your pets, or doing puzzles, are all wonderful ways to recharge from all of your awesome projects.

Now that you have a good idea of how to BASH your challenges, it's time to talk about how to develop good communication skills so that when you talk to others about anything, including hard stuff, you can say what you mean in a way that is effective and helpful.

COMMUNICATING WITH OTHERS

Communication is power. Those who have mastered its effective use can change their own experience of the world and the world's experience of them. All behavior and feelings find their original roots in some form of communication.
– TONY ROBBINS

All of the successful women we interviewed agreed that one of the most important qualities to have is the ability to communicate well. In life, and in business, how well you listen to others and get your point across when you speak can lead to success if you do communicate well, and failure if you don't.

STEAM-powered girls and women use successful communication to become more powerful in all that they do. You have an opportunity every day to use your intelligence, your ears, and your mouth to make a positive impact. Just like any other skill, learning to communicate well takes the willingness to learn and the dedication to practice.

We have two ears and one mouth so that we can listen twice as much as we speak.
– EPICTETUS, GREEK PHILOSOPHER

Alexandra Sanz-Guerrero says, "When I first became a test lead for a project, I was only twenty-five years old, and I led a team of ten or more people through a series of tests. Most of the team was respectful and welcomed me as a new addition to the team, but there were a few who made it clear they were not interested in listening to such a young woman tell them the best way to test their systems.

"We struggled a lot as a team. The first series of tests weren't successful, and it was highly stressful for me. I started to hate my job and regret taking the new position and title. I talked to people in the office about how to handle the difficult personalities I was working with. We finally made it through the last test in the series, and we worked through the test together as a team.

"After the test, the team members who disrespected me the most at last saw the benefit I offered the team. Now when I work with them, they are a lot nicer and pay attention when I offer my opinion. It took perseverance to make it through and to not quit, but with the help of my senior coworkers, my closest friends, and my own determination, I was able to keep going and make it through. I'm now happy I stuck through it, because it taught me how to deal with people, how to ask better questions, and how to get the most out of a difficult team."

Jessica Vineyard tells this story of the importance of good communication skills: "The best advice I ever got was from a dear friend of mine. Many years ago she emphasized how important it is to be a good communicator. Even as a mature adult I was afraid of having difficult discussions with others. She helped me see that pushing through the fear of having these conversations, and being diplomatic while doing so, usually results in a positive outcome and develops a stronger trust between two people, no matter who they are."

Having difficult conversations can be scary, but pushing through the fear, and being kind and respectful while doing so, can lead to better outcomes and more trust between people.

▶▶▶ *Jennifer: I used to talk a lot because I was nervous and didn't know what to say, so I just filled the time with chatter. One of my favorite English teachers took me aside one day and gave me advice about communicating and being effective when I speak.*

She offered to teach me a few tricks to have people listen to what I had to say instead of tuning me out.

The first thing she suggested was to spend time paying attention to people and how they listened to others. How long did they listen before they butted in with their own words? She asked me to watch their reactions when friends cut them off before they finished what they were saying. At first, I thought it was odd that my teacher was teaching me how to communicate (talk) by paying attention to listening (not talk); I thought that she was going to teach me how to use words more efficiently. Since she was taking extra time to do this with me, I went along. You should try it, too. It's an interesting and eye-opening exercise.

Next, she asked me to pay attention to how people whom I respected and liked listening to spoke. What I noticed was that they didn't react right away; they took their time to think about what they were saying. They also spoke more slowly than everyone else, like they were really thinking about what they were saying and not just rattling on. What they said seemed more intelligent, and sometimes funnier.

My teacher told me that the part of the brain that reacts emotionally (the amygdala) fires up much faster than the part of the brain that thinks (the frontal lobe). The average human response time is less than one second, but it takes at least ten seconds to think of a response and another ten seconds to put it into motion. People who are effective communicators (and who get in less trouble for what comes out of their mouths) take time to breathe slowly for ten seconds before they respond to challenging situations. ◀◀

WHO SOLVES THE PROBLEM THE BEST?

▶▶ *Jennifer: Sara and I decided to play a game to give you some ideas on how to deal with people. We all have to deal with parents, other girls, boys, teachers, and other adults. We have parents who love us even when they are frustrated or upset with us, just as we love them when we are frustrated or upset with them. The problem is that they think they know and understand everything that is happening in our lives. They think they know our friends, what we should study in school, where and when we should go, what time we should be back, what kind of clothes and haircuts we should have, and the list goes on and on.*

This is how we will play the game: Sara and I will describe situations with someone we all have to deal with, and then we will both come up with solutions. You then pick which one you think is the best solution for you. You can also add your own solution by writing it in your journal. ◀◀

OTHER GIRLS

Situation: You are with a group of girls talking in the cafeteria after lunch, and the subject of going to the movies this Friday comes up. Two of the girls decide not to include Theresa, one of the girls that you all hang out with. The girls who want to exclude her think Theresa is kind of nerdy and doesn't dress the way that most of the other girls in school dress. They say that she sometimes embarrasses them with her clothes.

Problem: You feel bad because you like Theresa, but you are afraid that if you stick up for her, then you'll be next.

Solution:

▶▶ Sara: It's uncomfortable being around a group of girls when they are talking about another girl, especially one you like. In the past, I've stuck up for the girl who wasn't there and told the group that they were being mean. One time they told me that if I didn't like it, I could go with her by myself. From then on, they never invited me to go with them.

In this case with Theresa, I could keep my mouth shut, not say anything bad or mean, and just go with the other girls to the movies on Friday. I can't change other people's opinions. They weren't being bullies or anything, they were just choosing not to invite someone. Theresa didn't know what they were saying about her.

I could also invite Theresa to go to the movies with me on Saturday. I like the other girls, but I also like Theresa. The other girls don't have to invite anyone they don't want to, but I also don't want Theresa to feel excluded. I would just hang out with her and the other girls at different times. ◀◀◀

▶▶▶   *Jennifer: I have been working on the BASH process and practicing the things my teacher told me about. While the girls go on and on about what the "right clothes" would be for Friday night, I would take a couple of deep breaths and think of how I would feel if I were Theresa and was not invited to go with our group, which she is usually a part of. Feeling excluded is not a fun feeling.*

Knowing that my brain responds to emotions before the part that thinks, first I would not blurt out how mean they were being to try to make them feel guilty. I would count to ten, and think of how I could point out to them that it could really hurt Theresa's feelings if she found out later that she was left out. I would know deep down inside that my friends were not going out of their way to be bullies or make Theresa feel bad, but sometimes that's what happens without thinking.

My solution would be to point out that sometimes I dress differently depending on how I feel at the moment, and that the way new styles get started is by someone being daring enough to do something different. Maybe we could invite Theresa and talk about different styles and use a few of her choices to add to what we already have. I might point out that Theresa tends to be smarter than the rest of us in the classroom, and that we could ask her to share some of her tricks to making good grades. We could also offer her a few pointers to make her look even prettier.

As my English teacher pointed out, we don't have to make others wrong when we offer alternate ideas. That way they don't have to be defensive over ideas that might not be the best at the time. This way it can be a win-win. ◀◀◀

A person who has someone's best interests at heart communicates with kindness and compassion. They ask themselves, Is it kind? Is it helpful? Is it encouraging? If it is all three of these things, then it is a good communication.

Communicating socially is an imperative part of our daily lives and relationships. When we can interpret and interact with the emotions of others, we are able to build stronger relationships.
– SALMA STOCKDALE

TEACHERS AND OTHER ADULTS

Situation: At school there was a poster for a competition to design and build a drone. How cool would that be? We went to science teacher Mr. Radich's room at lunch time, said that we were excited about the competition, and asked if we could join a team. Mr. Radich laughed at us and said that we had never been in any of the science or engineering clubs, so we should go and find a competition that we were better suited for, like an art competition.

Problem: Mr. Radich underestimates you because you're a girl.

▶▶▶   *Jennifer: When Mr. Radich said this, I was shocked and immediately wanted to scream. Sara pulled my hand and brought me back to my senses. (I reminded myself of what I had learned about the brain: the part that reacts with emotion fires up in less than a second, and the part that thinks takes about ten seconds). I turned around, pretended to look out the window, and took a couple of deep breaths. While I was doing that, Sara politely asked Mr. Radich if it was too late to make an entry. He waved her off but said that the deadline to register was a week away, and then we would have three weeks to design it. Luckily the bell rang, and we had to go to our next class. We politely thanked him and left.*

Sara and I agreed to meet after school to see what we would do. ◀◀◀

Solution:

▶▶▶   Sara: I think it would be fun to show Mr. Radich that girls can do things just as well as boys and that we have the ability to compete in more than just art competitions. I love art, but I also like science and technology. I think all three go together. It would be fun to get a group of my friends together, download the registration form, and get started. There are plenty of teachers that would enjoy helping us with this. In fact, an all-girls team would be fun! We could incorporate science, technology, and art in the design.

My brother's jokes about female drivers also make me want to design a drone and learn how to fly it. I think it would be fun. Also, it could be a good addition to my talent stack. Perhaps building and flying drones is my next favorite interest or talent. Even if it isn't, I will have a wonderful new experience where I learn a lot about science, technology, and myself. ◀◀◀

▶▶▶ *Jennifer: It really makes me mad when someone thinks I can't do something just because I'm a girl. I know that a long time ago people used to think like that, and I always felt bad for girls who had to put up with it. I didn't know that there are still people who think like that, especially a teacher!*

I think the BASH process would help me out here, especially since I'm still mad about Mr. Radich's response. If the people at NASA and other great places use a process like that to come up with solutions, then I can, too. Breathe, breathe, breathe. I feel better now, and I have more than one reason to compete: first, because I want to (imagine me flying a drone!), and second, to show Mr. Radich and anyone else who thinks like he does that girls can do anything they put their minds to.

I'm pretty busy with other projects, so starting a team and learning all about drones doesn't fit into what I have time for, so maybe I should find out how many teams there are and see if I like one of the teams. If I do, then I'll ask them if I can join. ◀◀◀

PARENTS

Situation: Our school is planning a field trip to NASA's Kennedy Space Center in a couple of months. Of course, we want to go, and it didn't even occur to us that our parents would object. It's school, it's space and technology, and all of our friends are going. It's a no-brainer. Guess what? Dad said no! And Mom is going along with him.

Problem: Learning how to communicate and deal with parents is a lifelong process. Sometimes it's easier than other times, but the bottom line is that when they don't understand our situation, they put restrictions on us and think they know the whole story and what's best. We love them like crazy, but there are times when they *make* us crazy. We both feel the same way about our parents: we love them, but sometimes they don't get us.

Solution:

▶▶▶ *Jennifer: The last time I had a situation like this, I really messed up. I got mad and slammed my bedroom door, a big no-no in our house. That made things worse. When I came out, not only was I not allowed to go where I wanted to go, but I was also grounded for a week for slamming my door.*

When I brought up the idea of going to NASA's Kennedy Space Center on a field trip, at first my parents both thought it was a good idea. When I told them it was an overnight trip with girls and boys going, my dad immediately said, "No way!" I asked him why, and he said, "Because I said so." I then looked at my mom, and she just raised her eyebrows and said, "I agree." I was upset and confused. At first they thought the school field trip was a good idea, but then, when they found out it was an overnight trip, they immediately refused to let me go. I decided that they were not going to change their minds if I argued with them right then and there, so after dinner, I went to my room, acted like I was one of those female leaders on one of my favorite TV shows, and set to work.

I got out some paper and drew a line down the center. At the top left side I wrote "Reasons not to let her go." On the right side I wrote "Reasons to let her go." I put myself in my parents' shoes and started making a list of reasons not to let me go. The first things I wanted to put down weren't fair to my parents ("because we want to torture her, because we don't like space"). After I got that out of my system, I started writing down ideas that I thought were valid objections my parents might have. I came up with four relatively good ones, such as "because we aren't comfortable with you going on an overnight trip at your age." Then, on the right side of the page, I came up with some good responses to their objections, such as, "I am responsible with my schoolwork and extracurricular responsibilities, and I make good choices when I hang out after school with my friends." I went to the living room and asked them if we could sit down at the dining room table and talk about something. They both agreed.

I told them that I really wanted to go see the Space Center. I have always loved space-related things like planets, stars, space travel, rockets, and all of that cool stuff. I explained that I understood that they only want to protect me and weren't trying to think of ways to torture me. My dad laughed his evil laugh, which made us all laugh. It turned the moment into something less stressful when we laughed together.

I went through the list of what I thought could be their reasons for not letting me go on the trip. I saw them slightly nodding their heads. Then I started going through my list of good reasons to go, also addressing their objections. I think that because I was organized and that I looked at the situation from their side, they were more open to rethinking their denial of permission for me to travel with my friends.

My English teacher gave me another piece of advice when she was teaching me ways to communicate more effectively. She said that successful negotiators, who have to be good communicators, present their ideas and then stop talking. She said it is a sign of empowerment. So, after I finished what I wanted to say, I just sat there looking at them, waiting for them to respond. They both looked at each other and said they would reconsider. At least I got them to move from their position of "Absolutely not!". As it turned out, the next day they agreed to let me go, and were very proud of how responsible and thoughtful my reaction was to their initial refusal. ◀◀◀

▶▶▶ Sara: I haven't gotten the hang of negotiating with my parents as well as I would like, but this is my solution. I was at my friend Bella's house, and she was talking to her mom about the trip. Her mom was excited about it and said she had been asked to be a chaperone.

It occurred to me that since my mom likes Bella's mom and allows me to hang out at their house, I would ask Bella's mom to call my mom and let her know that she was going to be one of the chaperones. I figured that it would open the door to my asking if my parents would feel better letting me go knowing that Bella's mom would be with us the whole time. ◀◀◀

BOYS

Situation: Talking with boys used to be just like talking to our other friends, joking around and thinking alike, for the most part. Now they seem like aliens. Boys tend to be less complicated and less emotionally reactive than girls. They like to be complimented about things they do rather than on good qualities that they exhibit.

Problem: Dealing with boys seems to be such a problem all of a sudden.

Solution:

▶▶▶ *Jennifer: Sometimes I really like being around boys and we have fun, but other times I feel like I swallowed my tongue, or I think they're just kind of stupid. I know that it's not nice to say those things, especially the "stupid" remark, but I'm being honest.*

Boys are fun, silly, smart, confounding, simple, and so much more. They are definitely different from girls, and as I get older, I can see this more and more. I know that dealing with boys is and has to be absolutely, positively different from how I deal with girls. As soon as I realized this simple fact, my life became easier, at least when it comes to dealing with boys.

I believe that when I am in touch with my strengths and my talent stack—all the good things that make me, me—I exude a confidence that positively affects people, boys and girls alike. I believe that when I am strong they take notice, and even when they seem to not like it, they do like to see girls express their power in a way that is different from the way they express themselves. When I come across boys who want to prove something, like they are macho, I remind myself that that kind of behavior is like what bullies do. They are insecure about themselves for whatever reason, and want to make others look less than they are.

So many of my problem-solving techniques go back to the simple things that my English teacher taught me. Successful people don't rush into solving problems or reacting too quickly. Breathing is key, as is remembering how wonderful I am. I know that if I stop, listen, and pay attention to what's inside me, I can find one or more solutions. Kind, compassionate communication is a win-win for everyone. This is so simple, but not always easy. ◀◀◀

▶▶▶ Sara: It might look like I avoid situations sometimes, but a lot of times I am looking at my surroundings and using them to help me solve my problems. When it comes to boys, I think I'm neither smarter nor dumber than other girls, but what I don't want is to lose myself when I'm near boys.

I know that I am a smart girl who is relatively pretty, and I have a fun personality. Honestly, though, sometimes I forget this when boys are around me, so I try to stay around one of my best friends when I'm talking to boys. I feed off my girlfriends' energy because it gives me confidence to be who I really am.

There are times when boys in my class act like they are the smartest ones alive and that girls can't do anything as well as they can. I always give my friends a look that says, "Yeah, let them think that for now. We'll show them!" Remembering who I am and all the good things that I know are true about me gives me the confidence to be strong when I am in the presence of boys—most of the time, anyway! ◄◄◄

▶▶▶ *Jennifer: The tools that I have learned in this book have made my life a lot less stressful. I am also more comfortable making my own decisions, and not basing them on what others think. I have learned to use the BASH process without even thinking about it; it is now an integrated part of the way I live my life. I have learned to depend on different people as team members, depending on what the situation calls for. For choosing classes for my junior and senior years in high school, I have a team that knows me really well. After discussing my passions and my ideas for the future, they will help me choose electives that support me.*

I trust myself now more than I ever did before, and I choose to be happy as often as I can. I don't let the opinions of others bother me as often. I know that I can do whatever I put my mind to, and if my passions and likes and dislikes change, that's no problem. I am in charge of my future. ◄◄◄

We hope that you take the time to invest in yourself, have fun, practice the STEAM principles and the BASH process, and use the tools to make your life as great as possible. The women who were interviewed most likely did not have these tools when they were your age, but you do, and we think you can be successful in every aspect of your life a lot sooner and with fewer problems.

As with any other tools, the more you understand and use STEAM-powered tools, the more proficient you will become with them. The BASH process can be a big help when you are faced with problems in every phase of your life. Please reread this chapter often so that you can familiarize yourself with the tools that can change the way you approach life.

CHAPTER 5
Your Future as a STEAM-Powered Girl

A key factor in pursuing a career related to the STEAM field is the desire to know how things work, to have an innate curiosity about our surroundings.

– MONICA DE ZULUETA

You are living in a time like no other in history. For many centuries, opportunities for girls and women did not change much, if at all. The female gender, as a whole, played a subservient role and did not have leadership roles in most societies. With little technology and no automation, a woman's day was filled with tending to the family's needs. Education was not a high priority.

Noble Prize-winning physicist Niels Bohr, known for his research of atomic structure and quantum theory, said, "Technology has advanced more in the last thirty years than in the previous two thousand. The exponential increase in advancement will only continue." And he was right: he made this statement before personal computers, the internet, and cell phones were invented and hugely impacted our lives.

In the last one hundred years, from generation to generation, roles have drastically opened up for women, and the job market is changing every day. Jobs and professions that we have no idea of yet will appear in the next ten years. According to Department of Labor statistics, 85 percent of the jobs that will be available by the year 2030 do not yet exist.

Your grandmother probably grew up when television was only in black and white and there were only three stations to choose from. Telephones were attached to the wall, long-distance calling was expensive, and the only way to get photographs was to take them with a camera that used film, which had to be developed at a camera store or pharmacy. There were no smart phones or computers, cars were much simpler than they are today, and girls had fewer choices for future jobs and professions. Not very long ago, job choices were mostly limited to being a teacher, a nurse, a homemaker, a secretary, a hairdresser, or a stewardess (now called a flight attendant).

Even your mom's life was different from yours in a lot of ways. In particular, there was not nearly as much technology, especially when she was growing up, and because of this, you have a much easier time handling technology than your parents and grandparents do.

Today, you as a young woman are limitless in your choices. But as wonderful as it is to have unlimited choices, it can also be overwhelming to choose what you want to do for the rest of your life. You can be an engineer, a doctor, a physicist, a business owner, a banker, a fashion designer, a pilot, an astronaut, an accountant, a politician, an artist, or a singer-songwriter. It is hard to envision any profession or job that does not depend on some kind of technology.

There isn't one timeline for everyone.
People do things at their own pace.
– ALEXANDRA SANZ-GUERRERO

Remember Your Dreams

Think back to when you were a little girl. What did you dream about becoming when you grew up? There were no boundaries. You had ideas of what you wanted to do, where you wanted to live, and adventures you wanted to experience.

Take out your journal and write down some of the cool and crazy ideas you had when you were little. You can even pretend you are interviewing your little girl self. Ask questions as if you had her right in front of you. What is your favorite color? What is your favorite animal? Do you believe in unicorns? Ask her what her dreams are, and what she wants to do when she grows up. Most young kids want to have many professions, such as a vet, a nurse, a hair stylist, the president, a singer, a ballerina, and an artist. They do not put themselves into a one-profession cubbyhole. Keep the interview going until you remember the way it feels to have unlimited possibilities in front of you.

Now come into the present time and day, and start fantasizing about all the things that make you feel alive. Do not stop to think about how feasible any of your ideas are. There will be time for that later. Would you like to be on a spaceship that is going to the moon or Mars? Would you like to be a horse trainer? A singer? A dancer? Keep writing and letting your innermost soul speak to you about whatever it is that makes you feel alive. Just like when you were little, keep your options going, and disregard any thoughts that limit your imagination.

You might want to be a researcher who discovers the cure for the latest virus or illness, or an engineer *and* a dancer. No matter how old you get, there is always time to add another facet to the gem that you are. The more energy, time, and talent you put into something new, the shinier it will get, like a beautifully polished gemstone.

There is no where you should be, there is only where you are.
– REV. VALHERY RIPOLL

Jessica Vineyard says, "Don't listen to people who tell you math or science or physics or engineering is hard. Don't become too attached to a career path, for as you see with my story, it can be a long and winding one. (I have been a hairstylist, a chemist, a business owner, and a book editor.) You will fall in and out of love with many subjects throughout your lifetime. Your focus will change. Your interests will change. Your passions will change. Learn to recognize the difference between a passing fancy and a deep interest."

IMAGINE YOUR FUTURE

No one can take your education away from you.
– ANGELINE GROSS

Who is writing your biography? Your future is in your hands. No matter what happens to you or around you, you have the power to choose how you deal with it. When things happen, do you get stronger or get knocked down? Do you fall apart when someone says or does something that hurts you? When something happens that you don't expect, how do you handle it?

A STEAM-powered girl knows that almost every career choice depends on being at least a little STEAM competent. When you were growing up, did you have a microscope or a telescope? Did you take apart electrical devices? What STEAM classes got you excited? Do you like programming, computer apps, and other software technology?

Educational consultant Stephanie Holmquist, recalls, "I was in the seventh grade when we moved from New York to Tampa, Florida. The academic track was quite different in Tampa than it was in New York. I was put directly into shop class, as that was the only class with an opening. I was the only girl in the class. I had an absolutely awesome teacher, who I have still maintained contact with. He didn't cut me any slack, and I learned how to use and be comfortable with both manual and power tools. Even more important was the example he set for the boys in the class. They saw that he expected me to do everything as well as they did, if not better. I think it was eye-opening for the boys. I know I earned their respect. I give a lot of credit to my teacher. That class really could have been awful. Instead, I wanted to learn more about technology because of it."

You don't know how many people you can affect. How we treat others not only affects them but also shows those around them how to treat others.

Choosing a Career Path

Now is the time to create a list of careers that are in alignment with those things that interest you.

Choosing a career path can be daunting; in fact, many people freeze like a deer in the headlights when you ask them what they would like to do after they graduate from high school. We created the following exercise to help guide you along the ups and downs of deciding what to do after you graduate.

This exercise is not designed to be finished in one sitting. You will be writing down your thoughts, ideas, likes, and dislikes over time. Throughout your life you will be presented with new ideas and opportunities that will make you rethink your decisions. It is really important for you to constantly work toward knowing yourself and being true to yourself. There are no "shoulds," and there are no careers that you must study just because someone thinks that you would be good at.

EXERCISE: CHOOSING A POSSIBLE CAREER PATH

*Envision a better future for the world, and
choose to be a part of making it that way.*
– UNKNOWN

In this exercise, you will have fun learning more about yourself and envisioning your future. Get your pen, paper, and imagination ready, as you are about to get to know yourself better and learn what makes you tick. You will be thinking about what you would like your future to look like and exploring what you want to study for a career path.

As with all of these exercises, start by taking some cleansing breaths, and then focus on what you are about to do. Think about each question. You may want to come back to your answers in a few days and see if you still feel the same way. Work on this exercise for as long as you like.

* It is as important to know what you do not want to do as it is to know what you do want to do. What do you absolutely *not* want to study after high school? Keep writing until you can't think of anything else. Once you start writing, you can keep adding to the list, so leave room at the bottom to write more things as you think of them.

* Next, write down fun things you do like to do and how you like to spend your free time. Make the list as long as you can.

* Look over the list of the things you do and do not like to do. Now you can research the kinds of careers that match what you have an interest in. For instance, if you really like

animals and love to take care of your pets, you might like to check out veterinary medicine or careers that support vets or rescuing animals. If you are enthralled by news about space travel, there are unlimited careers in this field, from being an astronaut to designing spaceships and future cities for outer space, to supporting roles that get people, satellites, and other technology into outer space.

❋ Make a list of specific careers that go along with your likes and passions. Are you interested in medicine, or does the mere thought of blood cause you to feel queasy? Does being a part of a team that designs and develops new materials for clothing excite you? Do you have an interest in transportation, such as cars, boats, airplanes, super-fast trains, or spaceships? You do not have to decide right now; this is the time to discover possible career choices. The more careers you have to choose from, the more likely you are to find the one that you like best.

❋ Interview an adult in the career or profession that you are most excited about, either in person or online. Ask them questions such as, What is the best thing about your line of work? What do you not like about your work and profession? Would you encourage me to go into your profession? If so, what would you suggest I do to be successful?

❋ Keep repeating these steps until you completely exhaust your ideas. Later, when you choose electives in high school, you can look at your list of possible careers and see which one jumps out at you. If there is more than one, choose the one that makes you smile the biggest, and follow that path when choosing your classes. If you take some classes and find that the subject is not the best one for you, then you can change your electives.

❋   Consider volunteering in the field you think you want to study. If you like engineering and robotics, you can volunteer at a summer camp that caters to those areas. If you like medicine, you can volunteer at a hospital or clinic. Make a list of possible places where you can volunteer in the future.

As a STEAM-powered girl, you are fortunate that in this day and time there is nothing off limits to you as a female. You are writing your own biography.

Many of our interviewees wrote about how they started in one career or profession and then were led to another path by life's flow. Never think that you will be stuck in a career path forever just because you choose it at this time. Remember that you are a multifaceted person, and it is your gift to be able to see unlimited possibilities for yourself. Many times there are similarities between interests and careers, which makes starting on a pathway of study easier.

It is never too late to be what you might have been.
– GEORGE ELIOT

Jessica Vineyard says, "I am self-taught in astronomy, although I learned a lot from hundreds of amateur astronomers by joining their club. My new friends encouraged and inspired me as I gained new knowledge about stellar evolution, cosmology, and all the wonders of the night sky. I eventually became proficient enough to teach astronomy to high school girls, elementary school students, summer camp students, elders, and community classes. I also founded and was president of the Southern Oregon Skywatchers astronomy club. Since it would have been difficult to become a professional astronomer in my forties, I turned my passion into a hobby that benefits my whole community."

It is never too late to follow your passion. Always continue learning and discovering new interests and parts of yourself.

Girls Can Build

After reading about all the amazing women you have met throughout this book, it may seem difficult to relate to them, or see how you are like them, because they are adults. However, everyone starts somewhere, and every one of these women was a beginner at some point.

If you want to build something, like a rocket or a robot, the best thing you can do is to start. If you have never built anything, you may not know how to start. You might only have an idea, a question, or just curiosity. That is your spark of inspiration, and the best thing to do is to start with that. In fact, the first step of the scientific method is to ask a question. You have already accomplished step one! (See the STEAM-powered activities in appendix C to get your imagination juices going.)

Once you have asked a question, the second step is to do background research. This can be as simple as doing a Google search, reading a Wikipedia article, or watching a YouTube tutorial. As you learn, you will have more questions and may even get stuck. That is all right; be confident that you have the ability to figure it out. If you get stuck, it is OK to ask for help. This is what happened to Lizzy when she built her first project.

Lizzy here. My first experience building something was for a science fair project in the seventh grade. I was excited to do a science fair project, but I wasn't sure what I wanted to build, so I looked through a binder my teacher had, which was supposed to help the students get project ideas when they were stumped. As I was flipping through, I saw a picture of an airplane. I remembered all the times my dad talked about airplanes and how much fun it had been to learn about things that fly. I decided to do my project on airplanes.

When I got home, I went to my parents' bookcase and found one of my dad's airplane books. One of the first things explained in the book was airfoils, which are airplane wings that are not attached to an airplane. I decided to do my project on airfoils and to figure out the best way to make them fly. During this project, I learned about "angle of attack," which describes the angle the air foil is set at, and "lift," which means the force that pushes airfoils up, making airplanes fly. For my project on air foils, I wanted to test which angle of attack would create the most lift.

I built five different kinds of airfoils. I also built a wind tunnel, which is a device that shoots wind through an enclosed area. Wind tunnels are usually used to test planes, rockets, the effects of wind on objects, and so on. I was nervous because I had never built anything before, and I was the only person at school who chose a physics project for the science fair. I was scared that I was not smart enough and didn't know enough to do the project.

You are always most nervous and uncomfortable the first time you do something. The more you practice, the easier it becomes.
– MONICA DE ZULUETA

I had seen airplanes, of course, and had made paper and wooden airplanes, but I had never built anything very complicated or that needed tools. So, I asked my dad for help. I knew he fixed stuff around the house and knew how to use tools. I also did research online and bought the materials I would need.

It took me a while to make everything, but when I was done and turned on my wind tunnel for the first time, I was so proud. The coolest part about building that wind tunnel was that it worked when I turned it on for the first time. I made it out of pieces of plastic, a fan, rivets (metal pins used to hold metal plates together), and a tripod, which is a three-legged stand used to hold something up. As the person who had put these materials together, I had made something come to life. It is a magical and powerful feeling to put together items that on their own don't do anything, but when combined do something incredible. I still get that feeling today every time I build something and make it work.

Learn from your mistakes and also your peers' mistakes.
– MIRANDA AUFIERO SMITH

Even though the empowerment that building gives you is amazing, it can also feel intimidating. I worry about whether my ideas will work or if I will make mistakes. Yet even when I make mistakes, I learn. All of my proudest stories are from times when I made a mistake and learned something. It's important to know that every time you make a mistake, you learn another way of not doing whatever it is you're trying to do.

Trying new techniques and making mistakes can be frustrating and disappointing; this is normal, and it's OK to feel that way when an idea doesn't work. Just remember that when you keep trying, you will eventually get the solution or result you are looking for, and all of your projects and dreams will come to life.

◄◄◆►►

*When you make a mistake, try to mitigate it and
learn from it, but do keep it in perspective.*
– ELIZABETH HILDEBRAND DOBBS

Mistakes happen, and acknowledging them is an essential part of addressing, fixing, and learning from them. But keep it in perspective; everyone makes mistakes, so once you fix a mistake, move on. Don't internalize it or fault yourself for making a mistake. One mistake does not equal failure; in fact, it is often a stepping stone to success.

CREATIVE CAREERS

The "A" in STEAM stands for the arts, but what does it have to do with science, technology, engineering, and math? The dictionary gives a lot of definitions for the word "art," but our favorite is from the *Oxford English Dictionary*, which states that art is "works produced by human creative skill and imagination." This means that whenever you create and use your imagination, you are creating art. It may seem odd to connect the arts and science, but some of the best inventors in history were both artists and scientists, including Leonardo da Vinci and Hedy Lamarr (see appendix B to learn about inventor and Hollywood actress Hedy Lamarr).

Art happens when you tap in to your creativity. Regardless of whether you express that creativity through painting, photography, sculpting, music, dance, or drawing, when you create art, you tap in to the creative part of your brain and your imagination. All of the ways you express your creativity act as your "medium," or the method through which your creativity is expressed.

Lizzy here. We builders, engineers, and scientists often think that we don't have an artistic ability or are not able to make cool or beautiful art. I had always felt this way, and it wasn't until my last year in high school that I learned I could use my robotics skills to make engaging and impressive art pieces. When I was a senior in high school, my school didn't have higher-level math or science classes; it only offered higher-level English, Spanish, art, and history classes. Even though I knew I was going to be studying engineering in college, I couldn't take any higher-level math or science classes. I liked history and worked hard in English and Spanish class, but I couldn't draw and didn't like to paint.

I had never considered myself artistic, so I was intimidated when I stepped into my art class on the first day of school. The class had only four students, including a girl who studied film and now owns her own photography business, a girl who went on to study art in college and now teaches art in her own studio, and a girl who transferred to my high school from an art magnet school. Then there was me, the engineering student who liked building robots.

I struggled the whole year. I didn't fill my art notebook because I never had anything to put in it. After Christmas break, our teacher told us that we were each going to be working on one big project during the second half of the year. We had to decide on a theme and pick a medium. I had no idea what to do, but I knew that I had to come up with a plan or I would get an F. I decided to concentrate on all of the things I did know how to do, such as welding, soldering, and working with metal. I had built one-hundred-twenty-pound robots before, so I knew how to build big, moving objects using lots of different materials.

As I was brainstorming, I thought about the materials I would use and where those materials come from. That inspired me to think about focusing on the four elements: earth, water, fire, and air. I decided to build a sculpture of Mother Earth. I made her from copper, an element that is dug out of the ground, to represent the earth element. I built a moving fountain and put two fish (like the astrological sign Pisces) on the front of it to represent the water element. I used a bandsaw, a jigsaw, and a drill to cut out a silhouette of the land on planet Earth, and I cut out flames from copper sheets for the fire element. I designed a power-generating windmill with two layers of blades for the air element, but I didn't finish building it by the due date.

I called my medium "Metal Sculpture." I had made all of the pieces myself, and hoped that I would pass the class. Not only did I pass, but the entire school loved my art. One of the administrators asked if they could keep the fountain after the end of the school year, when the students take down their artwork. Even after I graduated and went to college, many teachers and administrators still remembered my sculptures.

Sometimes we have a misperception of what we can do and what we can't. We think we know the limits of our talents, but the reality is that there are no limits. We are capable of much more than we think, and sometimes we need to be pushed completely out of our comfort zone to find out what we can do. We also think we know what other people think of us and that our perception of ourselves is the perception other people have of us, but in reality, we usually give ourselves much less credit than others do. I was shocked by how much everyone loved my art pieces but also glad I learned that lesson. I might not be authoring this book if I hadn't learned how many different talents I possess.

◀◀◀▶▶▶

Don't do what you think you are supposed to do or what other people expect you to do; do what you truly want to do.
– JACKIE GARCIA DE QUEVEDO

Start from Where You Are

I learned that hard work, enthusiasm, and the openness to shout your goals to people can make a huge difference in the opportunities that come your way.
– LINDSAY BARTHOLOMEW

Now that you have read this far and done the exercises, you should be in touch with the ideas, dreams, and imagination that you had as a little girl. Honoring this part of you, which will be with you for the rest of your life, is sacred. As you grew from that little girl to the young woman you are today, and as you progress into the woman in your future, these dreams, ideas, and imagination can be the foundation of who you become.

All of these things belong to you and can never be taken away. As a STEAM-powered girl who is developing into a STEAM-powered woman, you have tools to strengthen the core things that make you, you.

> *Women are natural-born engineers because they are detail-oriented, collaborative, and communicative.*
> – MONICA DE ZULUETA

From the exercise earlier in this chapter, you should have a list of careers and professions that interest you. Where do you go from here? When you have a list of ideas that you are interested in pursuing, it is time to make another list (yes, it really does help to write things down, not only so you remember them, but also so you can see your ideas come to life in physical form).

Julia Cherushevich says, "Every time I start something new, I feel some awkwardness and discomfort. I often experience imposter syndrome, wondering if I should really be here. Am I as good as they expect me to be? But that feeling passes, especially if everyone around me is supportive and understanding. However, if I feel uncomfortable on a team because my voice isn't being heard, my contributions are being ignored, and decisions are being made by whoever is the loudest and not who has the best idea—well, that is a toxic environment, and there is no reason to blame myself. I just get up and leave."

Who do you know who works in a field that interests you? Do you have a teacher who could put you in touch with a woman who works in that field? Are any of your friends' parents in that field? Has a guest speaker been to your school who you could reach out to? You can also see if there is a professional association in your area related to your field of interest. Often such organizations are more than happy to have one of their members come speak to young people about the ins and outs of their profession.

Monica De Zulueta says, "Applying one subject to another industry is an indicator of mastering that subject. It helps you to understand the trade-offs of technology. Technology is not the be-all and end-all; it has tradeoffs."

As in all things, start from where you are and go from there. The more you extend your research and interest into a certain area, the more you will find that one prospect will lead to another. This is just a fact of life. Once you start down a road, things will "just happen" to fall into your lap.

Professor Alina Trueba says, "In my life skills classes, one of the things we talk about is that there are two ways to reach your goals. One is the 'straight shot.' I use my husband as an example. He wanted to be a doctor, so he went to med school, then residency, then fellowship, then private practice. Done. The other option is my way: meandering your way to your goal. In part, I was not clear about my goals for a long time. As a lawyer, I never looked forward to getting up on Monday morning to go to work. As an entrepreneur, I felt passion for the work, but outside factors led to many challenges. It now feels like every turn on the road was intentionally leading me to where I am today."

KEEP GROWING AND EVOLVING

Focus on intangible (soft) skills as much as other skills.
Being collaborative and communicative are as important
in science as the research credentials.
– LINDSAY BARTHOLOMEW

We have talked a lot about the importance of always learning, how if you don't know how to do something, you can always learn it, try it, and work at it until you can do it. Expanding your skills and knowledge is very important. But you are more than just a wonderful, brilliant brain, so it is essential to continually cultivate every part of you. Giving back, helping others, learning about the things that bring you joy, and growing your team and community all help you grow and evolve your heart. There are many different parts of you, and they will change in different ways.

Lizzy here. I have always felt that mentoring girls, providing guidance, and paying forward the wonderful opportunities I had growing up is very important. However, I never thought of myself as creative, and writing a book is a creative process. Now that I have written this book, I see it as an extension of what I have always done, and as a way to encourage as many girls as possible.

Monica De Zulueta says, "My parents and grandparents fled the communist regime of Castro's Cuba. They taught me that the government can take everything from you, including your house, land, and business—with the exception of what is in your head and your heart. They taught me to study hard, and instilled a passion and love for learning, which led me to earn my doctorate in electrical engineering. They taught me that what you have in your heart, meaning doing good deeds and helping others, is very important. Charity and giving both talent and financial assistance have been key parts of my upbringing."

Amanda Davila recalls her educational path. "If my path of education were drawn in a beeline, it would look like loop after loop after loop. I am always interested in some new field, learning something different, trying something out. I went through medical school during a time when science was very important to me, but it didn't fulfill my artistic side. I went to design school and was able to exercise the other side of my brain. I ended up combining all of my knowledge into a venture of my own, leading me to start my own company."

Always keep learning, not only to develop your mind but also to develop your heart. Be grateful for the people and blessings you have in your life, and pay it forward by sharing with others your time, help, and talents.

KEEP LEARNING AND PERSISTING

To me, a good day is one where I learn something new.
– MONICA DE ZULUETA

STEAM is constantly changing, which means that a key component of working in a STEAM field means constantly learning. No one will ever know everything, so don't be intimidated by new techniques or technologies, or not knowing how to do something. A piece of advice that we heard over and over again from the women we interviewed was to always keep learning, be persistent, and never give up. Always remember that you are not alone. Whatever challenge you are facing, another STEAM-powered girl or woman has faced it and come through with flying colors.

Rachel Winsten says, "One of my biggest successes was obtaining the job I have today. It was always a dream of mine to work at my current company, in my current position. I applied for five years and received dozens of rejection letters without even getting an interview. Many times, I said, 'I give up. I am never applying again,' but I still kept applying. Finally, I got a phone call, then an interview, then an offer letter. I share this story with others to show the value of persistence and never giving up on your dreams."

A rejection or a no is not a failure. Keep working at your dream, even when you feel like giving up. You will eventually reach your goal and get that yes. Anything that is worth accomplishing is worth pushing yourself beyond your perceived limits. We say "perceived" limits because the limits we think are there are limits we create out of fear. Fear can stop even the strongest people in their tracks.

Cathi Cox-Boniol says, "I never felt very smart. I think much of that stems from the nature of education in the 1960s and 1970s and the fact that I wasn't allowed to learn in a way that maximized or even addressed my unique learning style. This came to the forefront when I was in the eighth grade, during that difficult year of transition. I couldn't even figure out what questions to ask in the classroom to help me learn, so I just awkwardly sat there. If I could go back and give my middle-school self some advice, it would be that I'm smarter than I think I am; I'm just smart in a different way.

"Teachers back then didn't know to differentiate learning so that diverse learning styles could be addressed, so I was never comfortable in the classroom setting. I always knew that while I might not be the smartest person in the room, anyone else was going to have to get up early to out-work me. I just let my work ethic drive it all. My work ethic has always gotten me through when I felt like I was deficient in an area. I am willing to work like crazy to achieve success and attain excellence. There's nothing like the feeling of knowing you made it in spite of the circumstances that were in your way."

Transition points are always the hardest,
and these are transition years.
– ELIZABETH DE ZULUETA

You have been given tools and information to assess any situation and understand exactly what you are dealing with, find solutions, choose the best solution, and implement it. This process can feel like a magic formula. Every single person who has ever lived faced challenges. Instead of allowing yourself to get sucked into them, you now have the resources to move forward in ways that help you to constantly evolve and become the you that you dreamed of as a young girl.

There is one more big secret that will help you as you move forward in life: knowing your "why," or what motivates you. You and you alone will know why you do a certain thing or make a specific choice. Shakespeare wrote, "To thine own self be true." When you are honest with yourself, you will know the real reasons why you do what you do. When you make decisions and choices from the desire for a win-win situation, you will enjoy a true peace of mind as you evolve.

Elizabeth Turner says, "Participating in STEAM activities at a young age is beneficial for anyone, no matter what field they want to pursue. Being in robotics built my confidence. It taught me discipline, teamwork, creative problem solving, drive, motivation, and even fundraising. I learned how to have grace under pressure, how to be a good loser, and how to be a humble winner. I definitely apply these skills in my career in a non-STEAM field."

Focusing on STEAM skills will help you in any field you choose. Throughout their lives, women realize that when they move forward by following their passions and their innate desire to make a difference in other people's lives, they feel more fulfilled.

Lindsay Bartholomew advises, "Don't be afraid to tell people what you want. Be passionate and enthusiastic about all the things you love and dream of doing. In addition to following your passion, also listen to your instincts. You know what is right; your gut tells you. If you have to adjust, do it. There is no such thing as time wasted if you are working toward your dreams."

There are many ways to make a difference in people's lives. Small gestures, such as looking people in the eyes and smiling at nothing, can have a huge effect on someone's day, especially if they are struggling. Your action might be the one thing that affirms for them that the world is a friendly place after all. As you go through your daily routine, act with kindness and integrity. Stephanie Holmquist says that some of the smallest actions she has taken have had untold effects on others.

Throughout your life you will ask yourself, "Why am I here? What difference do I make?" We are all here to be a part of humanity, and we all have untold opportunities to make a difference in the lives of others. As you know, you are unique. You have a specific talent stack and a circle of people specific to you. What you say and do, and how you do what you do, matters, every single moment.

At the end of each day, go over what you did during the day and note the things you did for others that had a positive impact on them. Remind yourself of the things, significant or insignificant, that someone did for you. A theory called the "butterfly effect" states that something as seemingly insignificant as a butterfly flapping its wings in Tokyo can have an effect on a tornado in Tennessee. Giving a friend a compliment might spark an idea for a solution, brighten her day, or just make her feel better about herself. She, in turn, might pay her friend a compliment, moving along a wave of positivity.

When you are reviewing your day before you go to sleep, be sure to block out the outside world and allow your spirit or whatever you connect with surround you and give you a feeling of peace and joy. You may find that before you fall sleep, or right as you wake up, you are inspired to do something. You might be inspired to take a specific action, receive an answer you were looking for, or get an idea for a new project. This technique opens you to make positive moves that support you in following your dreams and passions.

You are a powerful human being just by living and breathing, and you are even more powerful now that you know who you are, how to harness your talent stack, how to BASH your challenges, how to create your team, and how to apply all kinds of other superpowers that STEAM-powered girls possess. You have been given innate gifts and talents. You are living at a time in history that supports people's pursuits no matter one's gender, and now you have been given the tools and ideas that will allow you to choose what you want to pursue.

In the next five years there will be jobs, careers, professions, and opportunities that no one has thought of yet. Thanks to the imagination and creativity of magnificent people around the world, technology is changing at a rate that has never been seen before. Imagine what you can do with your gifts, integrity, and motivation to make the world a better place.

WHERE DO YOU GO FROM HERE?

You might have heard the phrase, "The sky's the limit," and it is figuratively and literally the truth. You were born at a time of unlimited choices and options. There are STEAM-powered women who have lived in space for weeks and months, and even more are training to live in space for significantly longer periods of time. STEAM-powered women have been breaking down invisible walls of ignorance for the past few generations. They have tried and failed, and tried and failed again, but they eventually succeeded and have paved the way for you and all the STEAM-powered girls that will come after you.

This is the beginning of your STEAM-powered journey. In order to keep your forward momentum, continue to talk to your team members, read about subjects that interest you, write in your journal the positive things that you do, write down your positive qualities, and note your progress, no matter how big or small. Record your challenges, and then follow up with how you used STEAM-powered tools to find multiple solutions. Write down why you picked the one that suited you, and how it turned out.

> *I guarantee that moving forward and trying will get things going, and you will see progress.*
> – CAROLINA DE LA HORRA

Congratulations! You are now a STEAM-powered girl. Now go out and conquer the world!

APPENDIX A
MEET OUR STEAM-POWERED WOMEN

We interviewed many incredible women in our research for this book, and you will find their stories and quotes throughout *STEAM Powered Girls*. We want to introduce them so you have a sense of the diverse careers and academic tracks they followed to become STEAM-powered women. We believe their stories will inspire you, make you laugh, and show you that they have lived through being teenage girls just like you, with the same problems that you might face.

Lindsay Bartholomew is currently an exhibit content and experience developer at the MIT Museum at the Massachusetts Institute of Technology (MIT). She works on developing exhibits for a new museum facility. She has worked mainly in informal science institutions (science museums, science centers, observatories). She loves finding ways to communicate science and engage all kinds of people in thinking about, experimenting with, and getting involved in science. She worked on an exhibit about extreme Earth environments (the deep ocean, deep caves, Antarctica) at the Museum of Science and Industry in Chicago. After this project, she was invited to serve as the science communication lead on an expedition to Antarctica. Her work on that project prompted the University of Alaska to invite her to serve a similar role on a research expedition in the Arctic Ocean, as well as subsequent polar expeditions. She received a bachelor of science degree with a double major in physics and astronomy from the Ohio State University, and a master of science degree in physics with a focus in astronomy from the University of North Carolina. She has also worked in science centers and observatories in Scotland and Ireland, including the Royal Observatory in Scotland. She volunteered as a teacher in Namibia, taught physics and astronomy at Kent State University, and contributed to the development of the Frost Museum of Science in Miami, Florida.

Ave Brouckaert has been a nurse for more than forty years. She started in an emergency room, and has worked in home health, fertility nursing, and as an outreach nurse serving the poor and homeless. In college, she studied general education courses and upper-level science.

Julia Cherushevich is an embedded software engineer and co-founder of PriveHealth, a cybersecurity company in the healthcare industry. She has a degree in systems design engineering.

Andrea Cornejo is an interior designer. She has a bachelor's degree in political science from the University of Florida. At thirty years old, she decided to go back to school and study interior design at the Art Institute in Fort Lauderdale, Florida.

Cathi Cox-Boniol is a career educator with decades of experience. She currently serves as the ACHIEVE coordinator for Lincoln Parish Schools in Ruston, Louisiana, and is part of the adjunct faculty at Louisiana Tech University. She began her career as a secondary science teacher, teaching in the classroom for almost seventeen years. She was known for her integrated teaching, facilitating a student-centered classroom where her students exercised their creativity consistently while developing solutions to problems through engineering design experience. Her classroom had the first computer in the district, which required a phone line installation so it could have a modem to dial-up internet. She has a bachelor's degree in education. She taught science at the middle school and high school level, and currently teaches science methods at the university level. She also leads professional development workshops for science teachers across her state, region, and the nation.

Amy Cutting is a scientist at the United States Coast Guard Research & Development Center. She is a physicist and oceanographer by training. In her current work as a scientist and analyst, also known as an applied mathematician, she spends much of her time doing systems engineering to develop and advance technologies. She has a bachelor's degree in applied physics and a master's degree in physical oceanography.

Amanda Davila is a dentist-turned-designer and entrepreneur, with several startups in different industries. She went to medical school to become a dentist in her native Costa Rica, graduating with a minor in dental surgery. She practiced at an American-owned dental clinic before moving to Los Angeles to pursue fashion and design. After immigrating to the United States, she earned a bachelor's degree in fashion design and merchandising. She then realized her passion for skincare, which led her to start her own skincare line, Good Skin Club.

Carolina de La Horra is an architect. She attended the University of Miami, where she earned her bachelor's degree in architecture after completing a five-year program.

Monica De Zulueta currently works as a technical strategist for Microsoft on its Federal team, covering applications for the military. Her main focus is on solutions that are cloud and analytics based. These solutions rely on technologies such as artificial intelligence and Internet of Things (IoT). She began her career as an intern at NOAA on the hurricane reconnaissance aircraft, where employees are often referred to as hurricane hunters. She would drop sonobuoys, which are devices that collect and send telemetry data, such as pressure and temperature readings, to the National Hurricane Center. After graduating as an electrical engineer, she went on to NASA, working on their embedded communications systems, which are used for the processing and launching of the space shuttle and its payloads. After NASA, she worked at Coulter, which makes blood analysis equipment. This work was focused on designing embedded systems for medical researchers. She has a bachelor's degree in electrical engineering, a master's degree in computer engineering, a master's degree in engineering management, and a PhD in electrical engineering, with concentrations in biomedical engineering, computational electromagnetics, and digital signal processing.

Elizabeth Hildebrand Dobbs is a licensed certified public accountant (CPA) and currently works as an outsourced practice manager/chief financial officer for physician practices. She has a bachelor's degree and a master's degree in accounting. She loves working in the healthcare industry and alongside doctors who have devoted themselves to helping others.

Caroline Loor is president of an insurance agency, Flinsco.com. She left college after two years to begin working in the shipping industry and climbing the corporate ladder. For several years she worked at a steamship company, but after being passed over for a promotion, along with her personal belief that she was meant to be an entrepreneur, she started her own business. She has grown her company into a thriving and successful business.

Debra Englander is a writer and editor. She earned an undergraduate degree in English and a master's degree in broadcast journalism.

Lindsey Fischer is a technical account manager at a software-as-a-service (SaaS) company. She is the go-to person for technical issues, and helps to ensure her company's clients are successful in utilizing their software to reach their goals. In her work, she regularly utilizes HTML, CSS, APIs, FreeMarker code, and other software tools to troubleshoot and identify issues that customers may experience. She attended the University of Florida, where she studied anthropology with a minor in education. She worked in non-profit fundraising for many years, then enrolled in a coding bootcamp. Soon after finishing the bootcamp, she began working at her current position.

Patricia Fors is a human resources (HR) professional at an engineering firm. She graduated from the United States Military Academy at West Point, where she completed a bachelor's in science. She also has a master's degree in human resources management and a Professional in Human Resources Certification from the Human Resources Certification Institute.

Xyla Foxlin is a mechatronics engineer by training but wields that as the cofounder and executive director of a nonprofit called Beauty and the Bolt. She is a YouTuber and creative engineering consultant. She has a bachelor's degree in general engineering, with a concentration in mechatronics and creative engineering, and a minor in studio art from Case Western Reserve University. She was the founder and CEO of

Parihug, a company focused on integrating emotions and technology to create a fuller digital experience. She has previously worked at Disney Imagineering research and development and iRobot. She was named one of Cleveland's Most Interesting People 2017, Crain's Cleveland Business's Notable Women in Tech 2018 and 20 in Their 20s in 2016. She was crowned Miss Greater Cleveland 2018 in the Miss America program. Her inventions have been featured in *The New York Times*, The Verge, Mashable, Google's Made with Code, and more.

Jackie Garcia de Quevedo is a singer-songwriter. She has a degree in psychology and a master's degree in liberal studies. She has taken vocal lessons with many different coaches as she established her career.

Angeline Gross is a senior reliability engineer at NextEra Energy Resources, the world's largest generator of renewable energy from the wind and sun. Her focus is on making wind turbines operate safely, reliably, and economically. She is passionate about mentorship and volunteers through a group called Empower Girls, hosting workshops to encourage girls to realize STEAM as a potential career. She also formally and informally mentors several younger women in her organization so that they can become successful staff engineers and managers. She attended the University of Florida and earned a degree in industrial and systems engineering. She also has a master of business administration (MBA).

Stephanie Holmquist is an educational consultant specializing in robotics and STEAM education. She consults with schools and educational companies throughout North America. She is also an adjunct instructor in career and technical education at the University of South Florida. She has a master's in education and a PhD in curriculum and instruction.

Dottie Fauerbach Lee is retired after a long and successful career in marketing and retail for the food and beverage industry. She worked for a supermarket chain and was a food broker for more than fifteen years. She attended Miami-Dade College.

Michele Loor is a board-certified surgeon. She works in general surgery at an academic hospital. She has two main specialties: surgical critical care and hernia surgery, performing both open and robotic surgeries. As part of her work, she teaches medical students and trains surgical residents. After completing her undergraduate degree, she earned her medical degree from Northwestern University Medical School and completed her general surgery residency training at Rush University Medical Center in Chicago, Illinois. During that time, she spent two years completing a Burn Research Fellowship. She then went on to complete her training in a critical care and burn fellowship at the University of Chicago Medical Center. After completing her training, she had faculty appointments at both Cleveland Clinic and the University of Minnesota. Her training and time spent at these institutions fostered her interest in the care of patients with complex abdominal wall problems.

Ramonita Martinez is a registered nurse with many years of experience, and a love and passion for her field and patients.

Ave Monaghan enlisted in the air force in 1971. In 1980 she became a law enforcement officer with the air force. At the age of thirty-eight, she retired from the air force. She earned an associate degree in data processing and was seventeen semester hours short for a bachelor of arts degree in resource management. She began working at UPS, where she was responsible for troubleshooting, software patches, and hardware and software upgrades. In 1994 she took a position with the navy as a network system administrator.

NEO is a retired certified public accountant (CPA) with thirty-five years of experience in public and private practice. She was the first female corporate officer of a 125-year-old Boston-based global insurance company. She was also a corporate controller and tax accountant for other companies. She has a bachelor's degree in accounting, passed the CPA exam, and worked with one of the world's largest accounting firms.

Lisa Roberts is an inpatient coder with more than forty years of experience in the medical records field. She has an associate in science degree from Miami Dade Medical Center Campus.

Alexandra Sanz-Guerrero is a test engineer for various navy systems. She is involved from the beginning of the design until it is completed and fully built. During a test event, she works with engineers and the test facility to ensure that everyone follows safety rules and procedures. She has a bachelor of science and a master of science, both in mechanical engineering.

Miranda Aufiero Smith is a forensic scientist at the Columbus Police Crime Lab in Columbus, Ohio, where she works as an analyst in the DNA section. She has a bachelor of science in chemistry with a minor in biochemistry, and a master of science in forensic science, with concentrations in DNA analysis, drug chemistry, and crime scene investigation.

Bianca Soto is a pediatrician. She was a resident physician in pediatrics at Nicklaus Children's Hospital, where she rotated through all aspects of pediatrics (outpatient, inpatient subspecialties, neonatal, and pediatric

ICU) and treated all ages, from neonates to adults. She completed her undergraduate degree with a bachelor of science in biology and minors in chemistry and psychology (pre-med track), and attended medical school at the University of Miami.

Ana Victoria Soto-Quintela is a cardiologist with subspecialties in general cardiology, echocardiography, non-invasive cardiology, and preventive cardiology. Advanced imaging in echocardiography is one of her passions, and she has achieved level III training, which is the highest level. She has participated in procedures involving imaging of the heart, non-invasive valve procedures as the imager, and open-heart surgery in the operating room. She earned a bachelor's degree in biomedical engineering, with a concentration in materials science, and then went on to medical school, a residency, and a fellowship.

Alina Trueba is an attorney by formal training but has a passion for education. She has had three careers throughout her life: attorney, entrepreneur, and now college professor. She teaches first-year students a student life skills course required by the State of Florida, which prepares students for college and for life. She has a bachelor's degree in English and international relations and a law degree. She began her career as a lawyer, then started a nonprofit because she saw a need to bring cultural arts programs to students in K-12. Her other entrepreneurial projects have also been connected to education.

Elizabeth Turner is an attorney who practices primarily education law, representing her county's school board. She also practices employment law and is an adjunct professor at Florida Southern College. She studied environmental science and policy as well as earth and ocean sciences, and in law school she focused on environmental law. When she was in law school, she was selected for a summer honors program at the

US Environmental Protection Agency Office of General Counsel in Washington, DC. It gave her the opportunity to work on national issues at the agency's headquarters. She was later selected to be a federal judicial law clerk for a judge in the US District Court. She has a bachelor of arts in environmental science and policy and a second bachelor of arts in earth and ocean sciences. She also has a law degree and environmental law certificate.

Jessica Vineyard has enjoyed four distinctly different careers: hairstylist, chemist, entrepreneur/business owner, and book editor. After working as a successful hairstylist for twenty-eight years, she followed her passion for science and earned her bachelor of science in chemistry at Southern Oregon University at the age of forty-four. She soon headed to graduate school in environmental chemistry, but left after a year to buy a high-end spa and salon, which she owned and operated for seven years. In her mid-fifties, she chose her next profession to allow her freedom to travel, and became a freelance book editor. This allowed her to travel the world full time for four and a half years before coming back to the States in 2020. She is also an amateur astronomer, and founded the Southern Oregon Skywatchers astronomy club in 1993. She has been a speaker, presenter, and teacher for many astronomy-related events.

Rachel Winsten works in the field of environmental health and safety. She is currently employed with a major theme park in Florida. In this role, she works to improve safety throughout the parks and resorts. She works in research, entertainment, and attractions to identify potential safety problems and mitigate them. She earned a bachelor of science degree in civil engineering, with a concentration in environmental engineering, and a master of science degree in occupational safety management.

Lisa Winter is a mechanical engineer at a San Francisco startup, where she designs and builds enclosed camera systems for tower cranes. She has worked on many types of robotics projects, from rapid prototyping a consumer product to competing in BattleBots and working on confidential projects. She also volunteers using her skills to help animals in need. She works every day to implement her STEAM skills across multiple industries. She has a bachelor's degree in art from the University of California Santa Cruz.

STEAM-Powered Women in History

Hundreds of women in history have made major contributions to science, technology, engineering, the arts, and mathematics. This list is a small sampling of these remarkable women. We encourage you to learn about them so that you will be inspired to follow your passion. Who else would you add to this list?

Marie Curie (1867–1934) was a brilliant woman. She is the first woman to have won a Nobel Prize in physics, and went on to win a second Nobel Prize for her work as a chemist. She is best known for her work in radioactivity. While she was in the process of developing the theory of radioactivity, she discovered polonium and radium. Through her work she also learned that radioactive materials could be used to treat tumors. She and her sister, a doctor, formed a research institute for oncology in Poland. Not only was Marie Curie known for her brilliance, she was also known for her kindness and generosity. She donated all her prize money from both of her Nobel Prizes to the organizations she worked with throughout her career. She didn't patent any of her work so that other scientists could expand on it and continue to make discoveries based on her research.

Irene Joliot-Curie (1897–1956) was the eldest of Marie Curie's daughters. When she was little, Irene was very good at math and, just like her mom, enjoyed science. She, too, became a chemist and a physicist. During World War I, she worked with her mom using X-rays to locate shrapnel in soldiers on the battlefield, and received a medal for this work. After the war, she went on to make scientific discoveries. She and her husband discovered that radioactivity was not only something that occurred naturally but could also be produced artificially. For this discovery, she and her husband both won a Nobel Prize in chemistry. She went on to show that women could be not only scientists but also politicians when she became the Undersecretary for Scientific Research, making her one of the first three women to become members of the French government.

Hedy Lamarr (1914–2000) is a name you might know if you enjoy old movies. She was a famous Hollywood actress during the 1930s and 1940s. She was born Hedwig Eva Maria Kiesler in Vienna, Austria, and later moved to United States. At the beginning of World War II, she wanted to contribute and help the war effort, and realized that she could help by using her scientific abilities. She invented a technology called "frequency-hopping spread spectrum." This technology allowed larger messages to be sent across airwaves without being intercepted or listened to by the other side. This technology is the basis for technologies such as Bluetooth and Wi-Fi. Her invention is considered so important that she is now called the mother of Wi-Fi.

Lise Meitner (1878–1968) was a physicist in Germany and is best known for her work in nuclear fission, the splitting apart or breaking of an atom. When nuclear fission occurs, a huge amount of energy is released. Her work was key in the development of nuclear reactors, which are machines that use the energy created during fission to make heat. She was a well-respected scientist and was nominated for a Nobel Prize forty-eight times, including nominations in chemistry and physics. Other scientists she had worked with did win a Nobel Prize in 1944 for work they had all collaborated on, but she had already left Germany because of the Nazis. Although she never won the Nobel Prize, she did win many other awards throughout her life. She is still considered a pioneer in nuclear fission.

Sally Ride (1951–2012) was an astrophysicist and the first American woman in space. After she earned her PhD, she learned that NASA was finally going to allow women to be selected to train as astronauts, so she applied to be part of the NASA Astronaut Group 8. She took part in two space shuttle flights and helped design a system using robotic arms that helped the shuttle handle payloads. She went on to become a physics professor and did many outreach programs that focused on helping and encouraging children to get into science. She also wrote books, just like this one, that focus on promoting girls to get into science. She really believed in expanding the opportunities in science, especially in space, to many people. She is recognized as the first LGBT astronaut.

Pamela Melroy (b. 1961) was a NASA astronaut, an air force test pilot, and a scientist. After serving her country in combat as a pilot, she decided to apply to become an astronaut. While at NASA, she participated in three space shuttle missions, spending over thirty-eight days in space. She has also been an incredible role model for other women here on the ground. After leaving NASA, she went to work for the Federal Aviation Administration (FAA), leading the office that works with commercial rockets, and then in the Defense Advanced Research Projects Agency (DARPA), leading the office that focuses on developing our military technology of the future. To celebrate her work and contributions, she was inducted into the United States Astronaut Hall of Fame in 2020.

Jane Goodall (b. 1934) is a primatologist, a scientist who studies primates, which are a group of animals that includes monkeys, gorillas, chimpanzees, and humans. She is best known for her work with chimpanzees in particular. Her career started when she traveled to Tanzania on a research expedition. During her expedition, she closely studied chimpanzees. Her research led to the discovery of many previously unknown aspects of chimpanzee life and challenged many inaccurate assumptions other scientists had about chimpanzees. Because of this, her findings were considered groundbreaking. Since then, she has become an advocate for chimpanzees and other primates, and a conservationist focused on how animals and humans interact. Throughout her life, she has received many awards recognizing her work with animals and her teaching of children and people all over the world about the importance of protecting the environment and animals.

Henrietta Swan Leavitt (1868–1921) was an American astronomer known as a brilliant, kind, and joyful person by all her colleagues. She studied stars called Cepheid variables and is best known for discovering the relationship between how bright a Cepheid star is (its luminosity) and how long it takes to change in brightness (its period). This discovery made it possible for later astronomers to measure how far away other galaxies are from our galaxy. Her discovery is considered so important that Edwin Hubble, whom the Hubble telescope is named after, said she deserved the Nobel Prize.

Shirley Ann Jackson (b. 1946) is a physicist and the first African American woman to earn a PhD from the Massachusetts Institute of Technology (MIT), a famous and prestigious engineering school. She is most recognized for her work with semiconductors, the materials that are used in electronics and all of the devices we depend on today. She did her research at some of the most important labs in the world, including Fermilab, CERN, and Bell Labs. Her work was used to develop technologies such as caller ID, fax machines, and fiber optic cables, the cables that allow you to get on to the internet and have good internet speed in your home. In 1999, she was named president of Rensselaer Polytechnic Institute, becoming the first African American woman to be named president of the institute and making it possible for her to continue to inspire young students, women, and minorities to enter and succeed in STEAM careers.

Roberta Bondar (b. 1945) is a Canadian astronaut. She was not only the first female Canadian astronaut but the first neurologist in space. She studied many different fields, including zoology, agriculture, and pathology, which is the study of disease, neuroscience, and medicine. She is a brilliant woman and a role model to many girls around the world. She started her work in space in 1992 when she became the payload specialist for the International Microgravity Laboratory Mission. During this mission she conducted over forty experiments in the space lab. She has many other interests, including photography, and is the author of four photo essay books.

Julie Payette (b. 1963) shows us that women can be not only scientists but also politicians and musicians. She was a Canadian astronaut who participated in two space flights, worked as a technical advisor for the Canadian Space Agency on a robotic system for the International Space Station (ISS), and was the chief astronaut for the Canadian

Space Agency for many years. In 2017, she became the twenty-ninth governor general of Canada. She speaks six languages, plays the piano, and sings for the Ottawa Bach Choir.

Serena M. Auñón-Chancellor (b. 1976) is the daughter of a Cuban exile who arrived in the United States in 1960. Like her dad, she is a doctor, and also an engineer and astronaut. She has worked on the Space Station as a flight surgeon, and invented medical kits to help the astronauts during launch and landing and on the Space Station itself. During her time in the Space Station, she did many experiments that focused on what happens to astronauts when they are exposed to space radiation. To become a flight surgeon, she studied as an engineer, went through astronaut training, and completed a medical degree and a special residency in the field of aerospace medicine. She is a wonderful example of the incredible and interesting things we can do when we combine all of our interests and talents.

Elizabeth "Lizzy" Magie (1866–1948) was the inventor of a game that I'm sure you have played, called Monopoly. She was a game designer, an abolitionist, a writer, and a feminist. In the early 1900s, she created and patented a game called The Landlord's Game, which had two settings. The first setting was called Prosperity, where the goal of the game was to make products and work together with the people you were playing against. The second setting was called Monopoly, where the player was supposed to build companies and take the other players' companies. Monopoly became more popular; in fact, it became so popular that another game developer took the idea, changed it a little, and then took credit for inventing the game. Luckily, in the 1970s, Magie's contributions to the creation of the iconic game came to light.

Alice H. Parker (1895–1920) was an African American inventor. If you enjoy being in a warm house when it is cold outside, then you owe thanks to her. In 1919 she filed a patent for a natural gas central heating system, which is used in homes and buildings and allows the entire inside of a building to be heated from one main furnace or boiler. Her heating system improved on existing systems and ideas for central heating. One of the biggest issues with central heating at the time was that there was no safe way to get the heat to all the different parts of the house. Her idea of using ducts to transport the heated air was a key improvement to the design. Alice Parker was a hard-working woman and a visionary whose ideas were way ahead of her time. Not only were her designs amazing, they are still in use today to keep us warm and safe.

Olga D. González-Sanabria is a chemical engineer and inventor who was born and raised in Puerto Rico. After she graduated with a degree in chemical engineering, she moved to Ohio to work for NASA's Glenn Research Center. During her time at NASA, she invented special batteries that are called "long cycle-life nickel-hydron batteries," which are used to help power the International Space Station. She later became a director at the research center, becoming the highest-ranking Hispanic at that NASA center. For her contributions to NASA and for being a role model to other women in the community, she was inducted into the Ohio Women's Hall of Fame.

Maria Beasley (1847–1904) was a woman whose inventions changed industries and saved lives. Although she is best known as an inventor and entrepreneur, she didn't become either of those things until later in life. In fact, she didn't receive her first patent until she was thirty-one, and was a dressmaker until she was forty-four. One of her inventions that revolutionized an industry was a barrel hooping machine, which sped up the manufacturing of wooden barrels. She also made an important redesign of the life raft. Life rafts originally were flat rafts made of wooden planks, but she wanted to make them safer, easier to use, and fireproof. She invented life rafts that could be folded and unfolded so they would be easier to store. She also added guardrails so they would be safer for the people in the raft. Twenty of her life rafts were on the Titanic, and those life rafts helped save 706 people. She also held many patents in the United States and in Great Britain, including foot warmers and devices to help trains stay on the tracks and not derail.

Maria Telkes (1900–1995) was a pioneer in solar-powered technologies. She was born in what was then the Austro-Hungarian Empire in Europe in the early 1900s. After finishing her PhD, she moved to the United States to work at the Cleveland Clinic, a nonprofit that funds a lot of scientific research. While she was there, she worked on a device to record brain waves. After leaving the Cleveland Clinic, she went to work for Westinghouse Electric (WE), also known for its research and inventions. At WE she helped make instruments that could change heat into electrical energy. During this time, she also worked on solar research projects with MIT. When World War II broke out, she decided to help the United States and began working with the US Office of Scientific Research and Development on a device called a solar-powered desalinator. This device takes in seawater or salt water and then removes the salt from the water, making the water safe to drink. Her desalinator was used on life rafts to help soldiers get drinking water while they were lost at sea. Her invention was used in the US Virgin Islands to give people living there better access to clean drinking water. After WWII, she decided to devote more time to solar energy research, and she teamed up with an architect named

Eleanor Raymond. Together they built the first modern home heated by solar power. This project was incredibly special because not only did she team up with a female architect, but the project was funded by another woman, a famous sculptor named Amelia Peabody. Telkes continued to work on solar power technologies and inventions, and received many patents over the course of her life. These inventions include a solar-powered oven and materials that could handle the changes of temperature in space.

Ann Tsukamoto (b. 1952) is a famous stem cell researcher. Stem cells are cells in the body that can divide, splitting from one cell into two cells, and then choose their function. Stem cells do not have a specific job in the body like other cells do, such as skin cells. She has twelve patents and has worked with many different types of stem cells, including blood forming stem cells, liver stem cells, and neutral stem cells. One of her patents stems from work she did with fellow scientists, which was a process to isolate the human stem cell. Her contributions and discoveries have helped further the understanding of stem cells and helped doctors better understand the different systems in people's bodies, such as the circulatory system of cancer patients.

STEAM-Powered Activities

W e have included some fun activities based on STEAM principles that we think you will enjoy. Check them out!

Build a Bottle Rocket

A bottle rocket is a fun and creative way to learn about pressure, physics, propulsion, and aerodynamics. Using the bill (list) of materials below, you can build a rocket and then measure how much pressure is needed to launch it, the amount of time it flies, its velocity, and the distance from the launch site to where your rocket lands.

Designing and building your rocket, cone, and wings will teach you a lot about aerodynamics. If you try different designs, you will learn which techniques, designs, shapes, and rocket dimensions will help your rocket move through the air most effectively. You will learn to calculate the propulsion created in the bottle by measuring the amount of water you place in the bottle and watching the pressure gauge on a bike pump.

When you are ready for launch, you will measure wind speed and the direction the wind is blowing. Learning to do this will teach you how to factor in wind resistance and its effects on the rocket's direction and landing distance from the launch site.

BILL OF MATERIALS (BOM)

* empty two-liter plastic bottle
* cardboard or construction paper
* glue
* cork
* bike pump with pressure gauge
* paint
* duct tape
* additional art supplies to personalize your bottle rocket (optional)

Instructions:

1. Build the rocket's cone.
2. Roll the construction paper or cardboard into a cone shape, then secure the ends together with glue or tape so it is stable and doesn't unroll.
3. Attach the nose cone to the bottom of the empty two-liter bottle with glue or tape.
4. Make the rocket's wings.
5. Cut pieces of cardboard or construction paper into triangles to form the wings.
6. Attach the wings to the sides of the rocket using glue or tape.
7. Wrap duct tape around the opening of the bottle.
8. Inspect the connector on your bike pump.

a) If it is a plastic inflatable connector, make sure it is large enough to secure inside the opening of the bottle.

b) If it is an inflating needle, make a hole in the cork the same size as the needle, then push the needle through the cork.

9. Pour one liter of water into the bottle.

10. Secure the plastic inflatable connector OR the cork into the opening of the bottle.

11. Place your rocket in the middle of the launch site, with the cone pointed up toward the sky and the opening of the bottle, where your plastic inflatable connector or cork is inserted, toward the ground.

12. Pump the bike pump until the rocket launches.

When your rocket launches, measure the time from launching to landing. Once it lands, measure the distance between the launch site and the landing site. This will allow you to calculate the velocity, flight time, and any effects from wind resistance.

Build a Tower

When you think of a big city, what is the first thing you think of? Is it the skyscrapers? One of the most important applications of STEAM is the design and building of these giant structures. They must not only be tall enough to include all of the people who are going to work or live in the building, but they must also be safe and stable enough to withstand constant use and environmental stressors such as storms, earthquakes, and heavy winds.

Building a tower with materials found in the home is a great activity to begin learning what it takes to build a real building. You will learn about physics, civil engineering, and material science.

As you build your structure, you will see how gravity, wind resistance, and weight affect it. You will learn how the method of designing your tower and its dimensions affect its stability. You will also learn how the materials you choose affect its strength, stability, and height. Try building the same tower with various materials so you can compare how the difference in materials can affect your tower.

You can also build many different types of towers. Click on the link below to see a tower project that you can build at home using materials you have around the house. If you enjoy building the tower, look for other fun tower-building projects, and experiment with building different kinds of cool towers and structures.

Find instructions for building a tower at the Frugal Fun 4 Boys and Girls website: https://frugalfun4boys.com/2013/04/30/building-activity-for-kids-straws-paper-towel-rolls/.

BUILD AN AIRCRAFT

These days you can not only see and ride in airplanes and helicopters, but you can also fly remote-controlled airplanes; helicopters; and drones of all shapes, sizes, and configurations. However, before you play with these aircraft or get up close to a real plane or helicopter, it is good to learn the basics of what makes these amazing machines fly.

When you design and build your own aircraft, you will learn the basics of aeronautics, aircraft design, and the differences between how various types of aircraft fly. Try a variety of airfoil designs, lengths, thicknesses, and materials. Compare how all of these factors affect flight. Learn the difference between how helicopters and drones with propellers create lift and how airplanes and winged drones create lift.

Follow this link to find instructions for how to build your own airplane: The Homeschool Scientist website, https://thehomeschoolscientist.com/build-an-aircraft-engineering-challenge/

If you enjoy experimenting with the airplanes and materials listed on this website, continue to expand your knowledge of various airplanes, airplane designs, wing designs, and methods of flight.

ABOUT THE AUTHORS

 ELIZABETH DE ZULUETA is an engineer, author, startup founder, and mentor. She first discovered robotics as a freshman, competing all fours of high school and freshman year at Worcester Polytechnic Institute (WPI) when she was a member of the team which became the 2009 BattleBots Professional Division Champion. She then assisted the team which won a NASA Centennial Challenge in fall of 2009, and in 2013 she worked with the Track C Team from WPI that participated in the DARPA Robotics Challenge.

In 2012, she graduated from Worcester Polytechnic Institute (WPI) with her BS in Robotics Engineering, and completed her MS in Robotics Engineering in 2014. After finishing her master's degree, she returned to BattleBots mentoring a team of high school students who competed when the BattleBots TV Show aired on ABC. Lizzy loves encouraging students to build cool projects and to see the impact these projects will one day have on our day-to-day lives.

In September 2015, she founded her first company, Zulubots, Inc., an education, consulting, and design company that helps schools establish robotics and engineering programs and consults with small businesses and corporations on how to automate and integrate robotic technologies by integrating existing technologies or designing custom solutions. She has worked with a variety of clients and differing industries including the flower industry, the cigar industry, and the beer industry. She has also competed in many pitch competitions and been recognized by Babson College's Center for Women's Entrepreneurial Leadership, the Miami Herald, and the Small Business Administration's Emerging Leaders program.

Currently, Lizzy is working on her second venture, DrinkCaddy, co-founded with her brother. This startup builds autonomous beverage delivery systems for golf courses. Her dream has always been to develop commercial robotic systems and DrinkCaddy is the culmination of that dream. Lizzy hopes to be a role model for young girls, demonstrating to them that one can always keep dreaming, learning, and discovering possibilities. Learn more about Lizzy at www.robotlizzy.com.

NOLA GARCIA DE QUEVEDO is often referred to as the modern day "Bionic Renaissance Woman." Born and raised in Miami, Nola majored in psychology after she was voted most likely to succeed in high school. Being diagnosed with severe Rheumatoid Arthritis at 19 changed the course of her life. Despite multiple health challenges, Nola attended college and availed herself of multiple educational opportunities over the past 40 years.

Nola's passion has always been to make a difference in the lives of others, especially young people. In the past 20+ years, Nola has been immersed in the world of STEM education, robotics and engineering on many different levels. She was appointed by two different Florida governors to serve on the Florida Board of Professional Engineers for two terms. She founded the United States Alliance for Technological Literacy and worked at the College of Engineering at Florida International University, engaging local educators and expanding their knowledge and understanding of Engineering and STEM careers.

Nola has produced over 10 national and international robotics and STEM events, where thousands of participants have gathered to compete and showcase their technological wonders. Over 20 years ago, Nola, her husband, Bill, and the extraordinary educator Alan Crockwell founded StarBot Technologies, one of the nation's oldest and most successful STEM education centers. StarBot has positively impacted thousands of students, families and teachers across the country with hands on programs, teacher training and extraordinary events.

Nola has created many programs for under-represented minorities, kids with disabilities, children of incarcerated parents and kids from all economic backgrounds. She recognizes that all kids need and deserve access to programs that empower them to develop their potential and live happy, productive lives. She raises the necessary funds and produces programs that reflect her playful, delightful and joyful expression of life!

Nola was the head of the first all-female team on the wildly successful television show BattleBots, first airing on Comedy Central and most recently on the Discovery Channel. Nola inspired, encouraged and educated many young women to pursue careers in STEM related fields through her participation in televised robotics.

In addition, Nola has been pursuing her love of writing and publishing. She partnered with her accomplished friend, Alina Trueba, to create a boutique publishing company, World Class Enhancements, which represents authors who write inspirational, empowering and educational books.

Nola has been happily married to her best friend, Bill, for over 40 years. They have two wonderful sons, a terrific daughter-in-law and two delightful granddaughters. Nola lives a very blessed life! Learn more about Nola at www.Granolascorner.com.